ROMAN
DERBY

ROMAN DERBY

Maurice Brassington

BREEDON
BOOKS

First published in Great Britain by
The Breedon Books Publishing Company Limited
44 Friar Gate, Derby DE1 1DA
1991

ISBN 1 873626 03 7

Printed and bound in Great Britain by Adlard Print & Typesetting
Services, Ruddington, Nottingham.

CONTENTS

DERVENTIO
31 Sept. 1721.

To Lutudarum

Chesterfield

Ricning Street

To Etocetum Wall
By Lichfield

Common

Crown Ale House

Paces

10 20 30 40 50 60 70 80

A grarvld Road over the Pastures

Dukes Head
Ale House

Little Chester
near Derby

The Pond

The Track

of the Roman

The Track of the Ditch

Foot Path

A Well

Footway to Derby

Well

Derventio Flu.

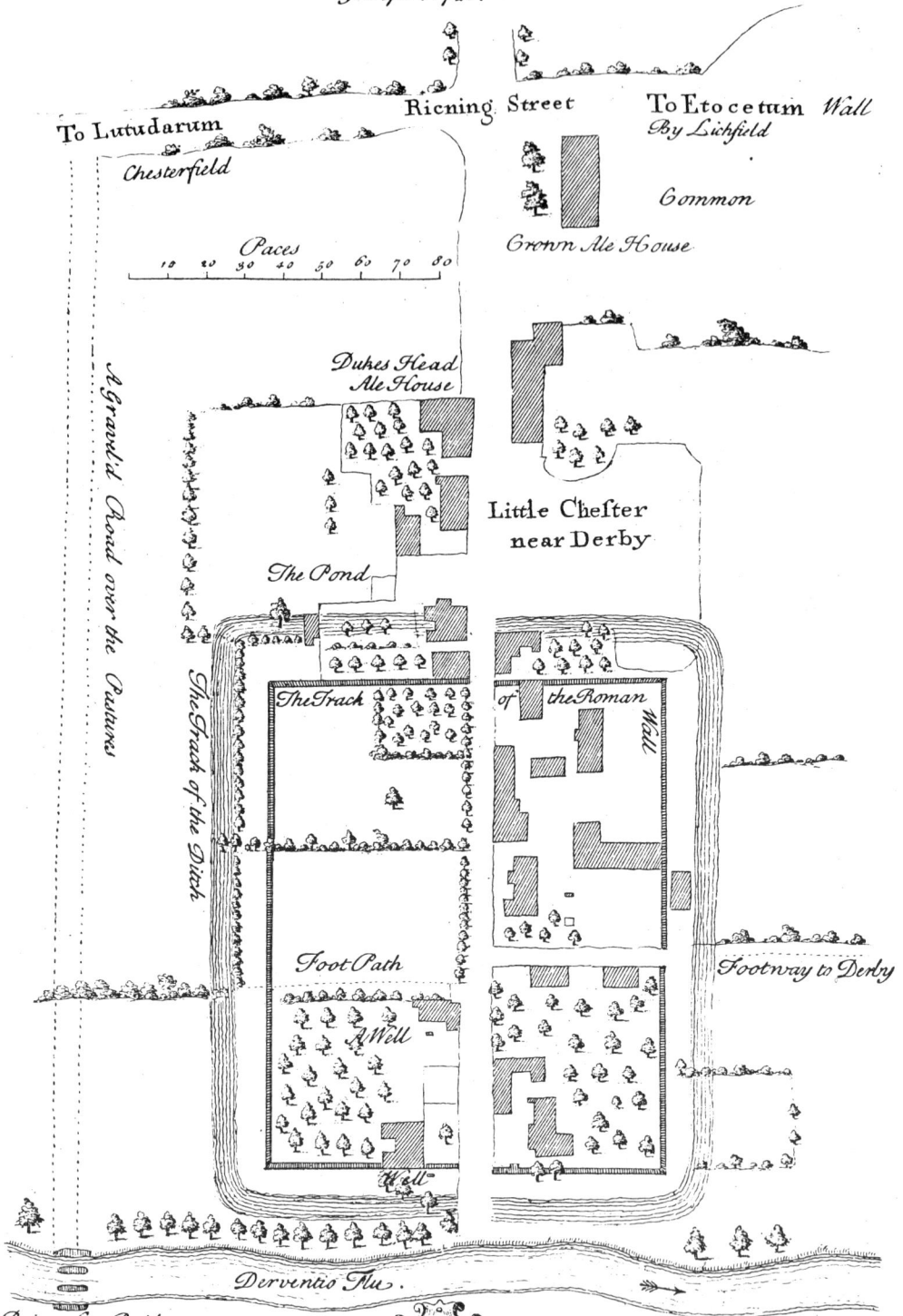

Ruins of a Bridg
over the River.

Simon Degg Ar. Castrum Roman-um jam suum d. d W. Stukeley

Stukeley's plan of Little Chester, 1721.

INTRODUCTION

I T IS not easy to imagine the streets and houses of the present City of Derby swept away and to visualize the countryside as it would have been in early historic times. The hillsides thickly wooded, in the valley bottom a Roman fort, and along the road a Romano-Celtic ribbon development.

Today, very little stonework from this era is visible above ground, and apart from the name *Derventio,* which appears in a seventh-century list of towns, no written history of the area survives and so knowledge of these early times can be obtained only by archaeological excavation.

The people who lived in what is now Little Chester did not exist in isolation and their way of life was influenced by what was occurring in Roman Britain and the Empire. Utilizing this information, an attempt has been made to trace the remains of the fort and settlement, and to reconstruct, as far as is now possible, the lives of the people who lived in those turbulent times.

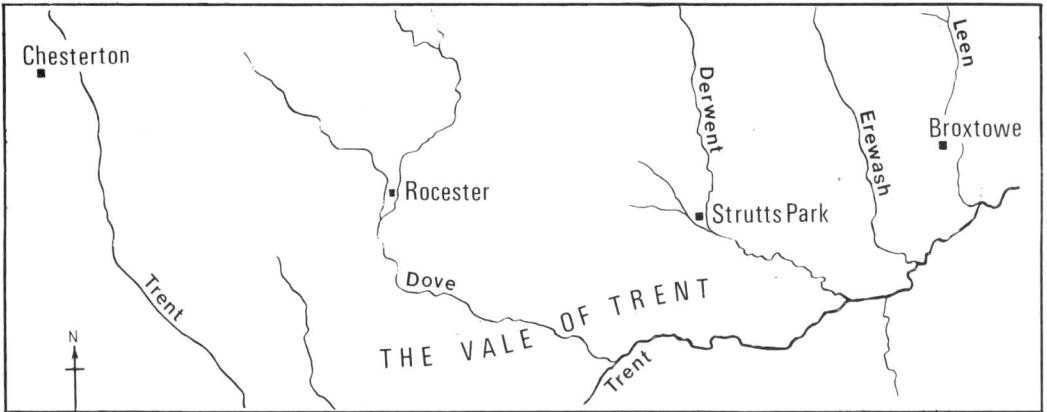

Figure 1. *Map showing first-century Roman forts in the Vale of Trent.*

PRE-ROMAN BRITAIN

CRISS-CROSSING Derbyshire were trackways already ancient in the Iron Age period. One of these, the Chariot Way, led from the interior of Derbyshire to the Vale of Trent via Bolehill, Alport Hill and the Chevin (this is the modern version of the Celtic word *cefn* meaning ridge).

At Milford, the Chevin ridgeway comes to an end and a steep descent has to be made to the Derwent. At this point the river can be forded (the old Mule Ford) and the trackway continues in a south-east direction to the Trent via Sandiacre and the Erewash Valley.

Another branch, probably the main one, ran southwards on the broad western bank of the Derwent, eventually following the line of Darley Grove, a narrow pathway between the high ground of Strutt's Park and the river. This gave access to the peninsula of land formed by Markeaton Brook and the Derwent which became the site of Derby.

After descending what is now Iron Gate and the Corn Market, and crossing Markeaton Brook, the track ascended the opposite bank on the line of St Peter's Street to The Spot. Here the trackway divided, the left-hand branch leading south-east into Leicestershire, the homeland of the Corieltauvi. The right-hand branch led to South Derbyshire via Melbourne.

Also leading to the spot was a trackway from Staffordshire, the territory of the Cornovii, which approached Derby via the Littleover ridgeway, Burton Road and Babington Lane. A continuation eastwards led to the Derwent where the river broadened out and could be forded *(Fig 2)*.

In January 1924, a Corieltauvian gold stater was dug up in an allotment garden near to the Municipal Sports Ground in Osmaston Park Road. This is the only Iron Age coin to have come to light within the city, although three Iron Age potsherds have been found on the Racecourse Playing Fields.

Another factor which indicates that Celtic occupation was sparse was a change in the climate. Pollen analysis shows that by 500BC, the weather had become much wetter and colder. This caused bogs to form on the high ground and marshy conditions in the valleys.

The area around Derby was, at that time, not well drained — the hillsides are composed of a heavy sticky clay (Keuper Marl) and the valley bottom was subject to flash floods. Since the population at that time was attracted to well-drained land, it is likely that no large settlements apart from the occasional farm existed in the area before the Roman occupation.

THE ROMAN INVASION

IT IS known from a fragmentary inscription on his triumphal arch at Rome that eleven tribes submitted to the Emperor Claudius soon after the Roman invasion in AD43. Although they are not named, two of them are assumed to be the Corieltauvi and the Cornovii, who occupied the land to the south and east of the Trent.

To the north lay the territory of the Brigantes, a large confederation of tribes who did not submit. Their boundary appears to have been the Vale of Trent, Sherwood Forest and the River Don.

Despite the fact that the Romans were on friendly terms with Cartimandua, the Brigantian Queen, sections of the tribe were not kindly disposed towards the Roman invaders and it was only with difficulty that Cartimandua managed to restrain them.

As a precaution, the Romans constructed a series of frontier forts along the Vale of Trent, connected by an east to west road. One fort was sited at Chesterton in the upper Trent Valley and the other forts occupied defensive positions on the northern side of the Vale, where tributary river valleys opened out into the river plain *[Fig 1]*.

These forts were placed at Rocester [at the confluence of the Churnet and Dove], at Strutt's Park [overlooking the Derwent at Derby] and at Broxtowe [adjacent to the Leen at Nottingham].

The Roman road linking Chesterton, Rochester and Strutt's Park can be traced through Mackworth village to the western boundary of Markeaton Park. If the line is continued eastwards, it will be found that it is roughly in line with Darley Slade, the hollow that makes a steep descent from Duffield Road, just north of Strutt's Park, to the river Derwent.

The early Roman roads were surveyed and constructed by the military for the convenience of the military; it therefore seems likely that the road would have entered the first-century fort on Strutt's Park directly by the west gate, a branch of this road descending Darley Slade to a wooden bridge supported by masonry piers [Stukeley's 1721 map of Little Chester marks two stone piers in the river].

The timber superstructure is an assumption, but it seems more likely than three masonry arches of large span, the river at this point being 124ft (38m) wide.

After crossing the Derwent, the road continued in an easterly direction, presumably linking Strutt's Park with the first-century fort at Broxtowe *[Fig 2]*.

THE STRUTT'S PARK FORT

CLAUDIAN coins, pottery and two brooches of an early type suggest that Strutt's Park was founded very early in the Roman period and named Derventio after the river. The fort was supplied from Letocetum (Wall near Lichfield) via a northward extension of Ryknield Street.

There is evidence that Broxtowe, the fort to the east, was of large size, possibly extended during campaigns against the Brigantes. The size of the Strutt's Park fort is at present unknown, but it is possible that it was also enlarged at that time to a similar size.

Derventio, comprising Strutt's Park, and later Little Chester, would have been garrisoned by an auxiliary cohort. Originally, these were irregular troops recruited from among the subject tribes of the Continent and they bore their tribal names, *eg* 'the first cohort of Thracians'. They were stationed on the frontiers and in the smaller forts and often took the brunt of any enemy attack.

The Legions, composed of Roman citizens, were held in reserve in the rear. Originally it was the Roman custom to allow the auxiliaries to do all the fighting and so conserve Roman blood. The auxiliaries, however, quickly became Romanized and were soon established as an indispensable part of the army. They wore the leather jerkins and tight leather breeches of the Gallic warrior, with a woollen cloak held at the shoulder by a bronze brooch.

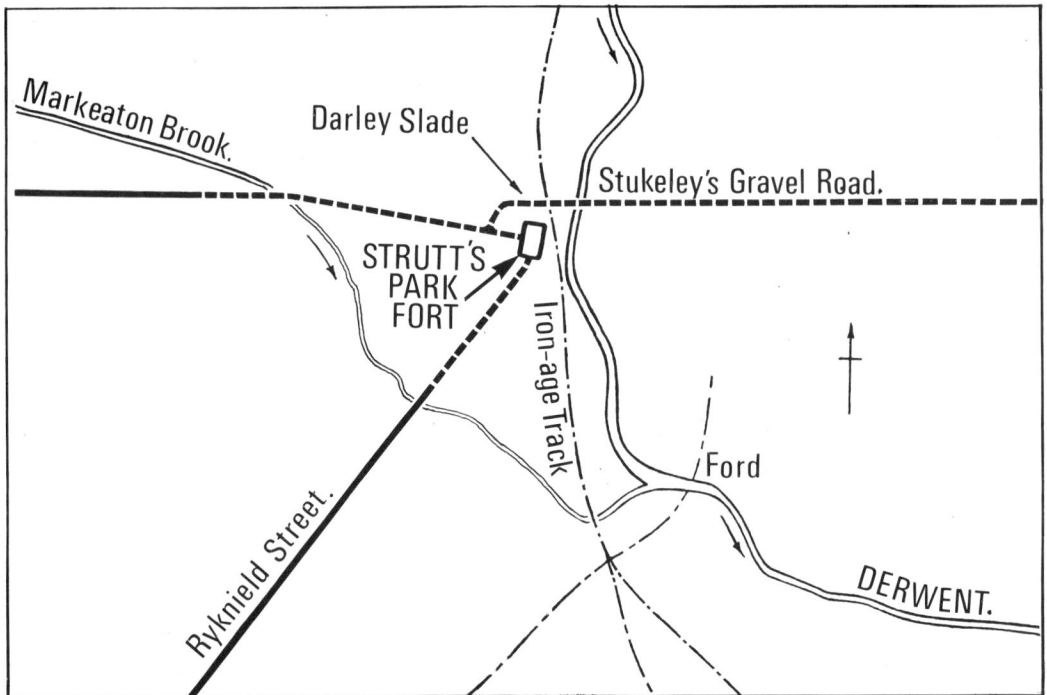

Figure 2. *Map showing first-century road system.*

Their armour consisted of an iron or bronze helmet, a skirt of chain-mail and an oval shield on which was painted the insignia of the unit. The sword, carried on the right-hand side, had a nineteen-inch blade, slightly longer than the formidable legionary short sword, the *gladius*.

Discipline was strict. A centurion carried a vine stick in much the same manner as a swagger-stick but, unlike the modern officer, a centurion would lash the back of a soldier for the slightest misdemeanour. One centurion became legendary for his zeal; after breaking his stick over the back of a defaulter, he would throw the stump to a subordinate with the order, 'Fetch me another', a phrase that quickly became his nickname.

A serving soldier could not marry until his discharge, but many took up with native women. These lived in the *canabae*, an encampment containing the camp followers and traders which the fort attracted. The army, however, did not recognize these liaisons and when the garrison was posted to a new location, no provision was made for dependents — they had to follow as best they could.

A soldier served 25 years and on discharge was granted Roman citizenship. Any children borne to him while in service also received citizen rights but his common-law wife, although now officially recognized, did not.

Although the soldiers lived in barracks within the fort, they had ample opportunity to visit their mistresses and carouse and dice in the places of entertainment which were provided by Roman merchants.

Booths were set up close to the fort in order to take full advantage of the free-spending soldiery. All the soldiers, especially the Germans, were inveterate gamblers. When dicing, three dice were used to throw the highest number: to assist in throwing a treble six, they were not above using loaded dice.

Other popular games were 'twelve points', an early form of Backgammon, and the 'soldiers game', which was a form of draughts. Gaming counters for these games have been found at Little Chester. A team game called *harpastum* was also popular and was similar to the violent football or hug-ball that was formerly played through the streets of Derby on Shrove Tuesday.

THE ICENI UPRISING AD60

THE Iceni, a tribe which occupied much of East Anglia, had been granted a certain amount of independence by the Romans. Their king, Prasutagus, hoping to perpetuate this arrangement, willed his kingdom to his two daughters and the Emperor Nero. Upon his death in AD60, the Roman administration considered that as he had no son, the royal status had lapsed.

Army officers moved into the tribal lands and began to treat the peasants and nobles alike as if they were newly-conquered people. Treasury officials with numerous slaves in the capacity of clerks and secretaries suddenly arrived at the palace and began to confiscate the contents.

The queen mother, Boudica, remonstrated with them, too vigorously it seems, for the Roman reaction was brutal. Boudica was stripped and flogged for her impertinence and her daughters, the presumptive heiresses, were raped by slaves.

The result of such folly was terrible in the extreme. The whole tribe rose at once to avenge this ultimate insult. The Roman settlers in the tribal lands were put to the sword. The Ninth Legion, hurrying to quell the revolt, was ambushed and cut to pieces, the commander Petillius Cerealis narrowly escaping with his life.

The Trinovantes, the tribe to the south, joined the rebellion and Colchester, a colony of legionary veterans, was taken and destroyed. The great temple of the Deified Claudius was burned with all who had taken refuge within it.

When the rebellion occurred, C Suetonius Paullinus, the Roman governor, was on campaign in Wales mounting an offensive against the Isle of Anglesey, an important centre of the Druids.

The Romans tolerated most native cults, but their clemency did not extend to the priestly sect of Druidism. Druids were magicians and soothsayers to the Celts. Human sacrifice formed part of their savage rites and Roman captives were often disembowelled and their entrails studied to ascertain the will of the gods.

Although the Romans sacrificed animals for the same purpose, the use of Roman soldiers was abhorrent to them. Thus they hunted the Druids down and virtually eradicated the sect. The assault across the Straits took place in flat-bottomed boats, the auxiliary cavalry swimming across with their horses.

Cornelius Tacitus, the Roman historian, describes a dense mass of men awaiting them on the shore with long-haired black-clad women, brandishing torches, surging back and forth screaming like furies.

At the rear stood the Druids, their hands uplifted, calling down curses from the heavens. This fanatical zeal at first overawed the Romans but, urged on by Paullinus, they beached their craft, charged into the chanting mob and began to slaughter priests, men and women alike.

It was while the troops were cutting down the sacred groves that news came of the Iceni uprising. Leaving the legions to follow, Paullinus made a quick dash to London with an escort of cavalry. He arrived just before Boudica and her tribesmen. Realizing that the city could not be defended, he left almost

Figure 3. *The gladius, a short sword designed for driving deeply into a milling crowd.*

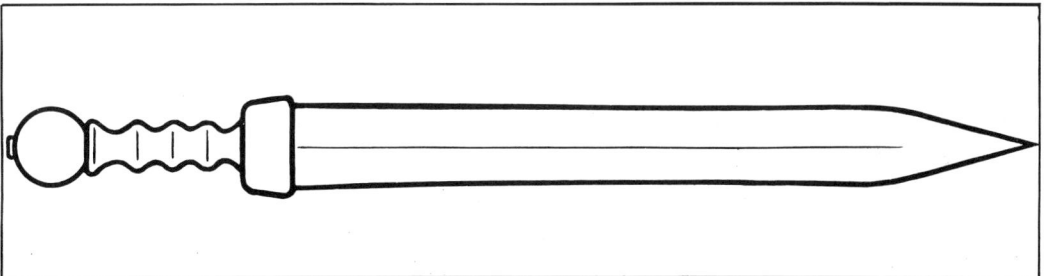

immediatley and Boudica put the city to the torch and butchered the inhabitants.

Paullinus retreated the way he had come, along Watling Street, a road now represented by the modern A5. Boudica followed him, pausing on the way to destroy the newly-founded city of Verulamium, now known as St Albans.

Many historians consider that Paullinus met his army returning from Wales in the vicinity of Atherstone, which lies some 25 miles south of Derby. Here he began to prepare the battlefield, since it was the Roman custom to fight on ground of their own choosing whenever possible.

An urgent message was sent to the Second Legion, encamped to the south, to march north and join the main army. The legionary commander and his second-in-command were away and the senior centurion inexplicably refused to give the order to march.

Paullinus had with him several auxiliary units, both foot soldiers and cavalry, also most of the Twentieth and all of the Fourteenth Legion. According to Tacitus he drew what troops he could from the neighbourhood and this must mean that the garrison at Strutt's Park was ordered south as a reinforcement.

Meanwhile Boudica's jubilant horde surged northward. Paullinus deployed his troops in a shallow valley on the flank of a hill which opened out on to flat ground, the dense woodland behind them ensuring that the enemy could only approach from the front.

The legionaries held a central position on rising ground with the auxiliaries on either side and the cavalry on the wings. The Celtic army, which contained many women, assembled in some disorder in front of the Roman position. An extensive baggage train carrying the wives and children of the tribesmen, who had come to watch the battle, drew up in the rear and on the flanks.

Boudica with her daughters traversed the field in a chariot acknowledging the various clans. The speech she supposedly made is recorded by Tacitus:

"I am leading you into battle not as a Queen by right of birth to recover my Kingdom and treasure, but as an ordinary woman, whose body was cut by the lash, determined to avenge her loss of liberty and the rape of her daughters. The Romans in their rapacious greed did not spare the old or leave the young unmolested. The gods now favour us. A legion has already been defeated, the survivors cower behind their defences while others seek the means to escape, they flee from a valiant people with a just cause. The Romans who now oppose us must realize that it is a fight to the death. It is my resolve that if you men wish to live on in slavery, I, a mere woman, do not. Follow me now to victory or submit to the Roman yoke."

The Roman legionaries, although heavily outnumbered, were very well armed and experienced men. They stood in close ranks, each man waiting to discharge a heavy javelin which had a long slender neck with a small barbed point.

At a given signal, some 7,000 of these missiles were hurled into the air, closely followed by a second volley. This felled the foremost ranks of the advancing Britons. The casualties caused by these javelins alone were prodigious. The momentum of the British charge was checked but the tribesmen in the rear still pressed forward against the middle ranks.

At this point the Romans charged in their characteristic 'V' formation, driving deeply into the milling crowd. The Britons found themselves crushed tightly together, unable to swing their swords. The advantage was now with the legionaries whose short sword, the *gladius*, was designed for this type of fighting *(Fig 3)*.

Stabbing through gaps in the shield wall they began their slaughter. The Britons were driven back against their baggage train and a general massacre ensued. The Romans spared no one: women and children were butchered, even draught animals were cut down.

Tacitus records that 80,000 people were killed. Boudica, knowing her fate, poisoned herself. After the battle, Paullinus did not disperse his army but kept it under arms and in the name of Mars Ultor, the Roman God of Vengeance, he began a reign of terror in the territories of the defeated tribes.

Catus Decianus, the treasury official whose policy was the root cause of the rebellion, had fled to the Continent before the Iceni advance on London. He was replaced by Julius Classicianus.

Roman taxes were always collected in full, regardless of famine or pestilence, but it was quickly found that the revenue from the tribal lands had greatly decreased since taxes could not be wrung from corpses. Paullinus was concerned with retribution, Classicianus with revenue: the two were incompatible.

Classicianus wrote to the Emperor advising that the Governor be replaced. Nero sent one of his personal administrators, a former slave called Polyclitus, to adjudicate. A compromise was agreed upon, but it was not long before Paullinus was recalled on a technically and a new Governor, Petronius Turpilianus, appointed. He brought the harassment of the tribes to an end. The cohorts returned to their bases and the country settled down to a period of uneasy peace.

CARTIMANDUA

THE Brigantes took no part in the Iceni uprising. Although the tribe remained independent, their queen, Cartimandua, adopted a pro-Roman policy. In an attempt to consolidate her position she had, in her youth, contracted a marriage of convenience with Venutius, who headed a powerful clan within the tribal confederation. Cartimandua was quick to assert her authority on behalf of the Romans when a section of the tribe came into conflict with auxiliaries in AD48. Later, when Caractacus, who had fought the Romans since the invasion as commander of the southern tribes, sought sanctuary with the Brigantes, she immediately handed him over in chains to the Romans to be exhibited in Rome. Her action is thought to have begun the estrangement of her husband and resulted

in the inter-tribal fighting of AD57 when first auxiliaries and finally legionaries were deployed on her behalf.

Cartimandua remained steadfast in her loyalty to Rome; had she, three years later, led her tribesmen down from the north to join Boudica, she might have changed the course of British history, but this was not to be. In AD69 she became infatuated with a youthful attendant of her husband. The freedom and authority allowed to Celtic women was always a source of amazement to the Romans. Some 140 years later, the Empress Julia Domna taunted a hostage princess at York, chiding her on the licentious behaviour of Celtic women. The rejoinder must have silenced any further reproach: "When we need a man our behaviour is better than yours, we select the best and consort with them openly. At Rome you pick the worst and are debauched by them in secret."

Although promiscuous, Celtic society was intensely aristocratic and Cartimandua's association with a youth of low rank alienated some of her clan and gave her aggrieved husband the chance to depose her. Venutius assumed that the Roman Civil War, which was raging on the Continent, would prevent any outside interference. Cartimandua, who was now in a desperate situation, sent an urgent plea for assistance to the Roman Governor Vettius Bolanus. Tacitus describes Bolanus as too gentle a man for so warlike a province but, despite this description, he followed the precedent of AD57 and ordered a task force be sent to aid the Queen. It must be assumed that this operation was carried out by auxiliaries supported by the Ninth Legion, then based at Lincoln.

The siege of Cartimandua was raised with great difficulty and there was much loss of life before she was escorted to the Roman lines. This action was unpopular with the army as the lives of Roman soldiers had been expended to rescue a promiscuous native female from her own folly. This dissatisfaction is reflected by the pithy remark of Tacitus: "A kingdom to Venutius, a war to us." The future Emperor Vespasian probably shared this opinion. He was familiar with the country, for as a young man he had commanded a legion during the Claudian invasion.

After his victory in the Civil War and his installation as Emperor, he replaced Bolanus as Governor with Petillius Cerealis, who ten years earlier had commanded the Ninth Legion during the Iceni uprising. Cerealis immediately led an expedition into Brigantia; again the attack must have been across the River Don in the vicinity of Doncaster. It is likely that there was also a parallel thrust northwards on the west side of the Pennines by the Twentieth Legion.

To counteract any out-flanking movement, troops stationed in the Vale of Trent would have occupied Derbyshire, Strutt's Park being an ideal base for such an action. The fate of Venutius and Cartimandua is unfortunately unknown, for although Tacitus records that Cerealis fought many battles with much loss of life, he fell short of claiming a complete victory. The Queen was presumably reinstated, but some of the northern clans managed for a while to retain their independence. A strong Roman presence was therefore maintained in the tribal lands; a fortress was established at York, which became the new base of the Ninth Legion. Some six years later, Julius Agricola, one of the legionary commanders who had assisted Cerealis, was himself appointed Governor. After a series of brilliant campaigns in northern Britain, which culminated in a great victory in the highlands of Scotland, Agricola had virtually subjugated the whole island when he was recalled to Rome.

DERBYSHIRE MINES

DERBYSHIRE, because of its mineral wealth, remained under military control. Lutudarum, a mining centre which is thought to lie in the vicinity of Middleton-by-Wirksworth, was established and produced great quantities of lead. So much lead was mined in Britain that a law had to be passed placing a limit on the amount produced. Over thirty Roman ingots of lead (pigs) have been found that are products of Luturdarum.

Because of the silver found in lead ore, the mines would have come under the supervision of the Imperial Treasury. Unfortunately for the Romans, only the mines at Cromford and Bonsall produced ore with any appreciable silver content; the other Derbyshire mines produced little silver. This must have been a disappointment to the treasury officials, who quickly leased the mines to civil contractors.

The Romans considered lead to be a by-product of the refinement of silver and it seems that although little silver was obtained, Derbyshire lead was marked EX ARG (Ex Argentum) to indicate that it was not bullion. Therefore, the inscription BRIT.EX.ARG found on several lead ingots can be translated as 'British lead containing no silver'.

The silver contractors who worked the mines were almost certainly freedmen, former slaves; their names appearing in abbreviated form cast into some of the Lutudarum ingots. These can be expanded to read Gaius Julius Portus, Lucius Arvconius Verecundus and Publius Rubrius Abascantus. However, the most important lessee was an individual, who is known to us by his initials TI.CL.TR., again found on ingots cast at Lutudarum. He is also known to have had mining interests in the Mendips and an inscription stamped on an ingot found in Somerset carries a more complete version of his name TI.CL.TRIFER. This can be expanded to read Tiberius Claudius Triferna. Lead ingots carrying the legend SOCIORVM LVTVD indicate that these four individuals formed themselves into a company based at Lutudarum, which after the death of the partners may have continued in business until well past the turn of the second century.

Freedmen, despite the fact that many became wealthy merchants, were regarded by the Roman upper classes as vulgar and ostentatious. Consequently there was little social contact. As teachers and scribes, some freedmen were highly educated, but for the most part they were trained to carry out only the task allocated to them when a slave. It is therefore unlikely that the treasury officials would be based at Lutudarum; their slaves would be there, but they themselves would be based at a place which had clean air and the military stationed nearby.

Only one site in South Derbyshire fulfils all the requirements and that is Derventio. It is thought that the ingots of lead were rafted down the Derwent or carried by pack mule; either way, the route would lead to Derventio. Roman masonry buildings have been found on the site of the Manor House Farm. They could possibly be part of a mansio (a lodging house for persons of rank travelling on Government business) or a base for the imperial civil servants controlling the lead industry.

STRUTT'S PARK AND THE COURSE OF RYKNIELD STREET

STRUTT'S Park, as a former frontier fort,

became redundant when northern Britain was occupied. Ryknield Street, which had ended at the fort, was diverted from the high ground and extended northwards to Chesterfield and Templeborough. This diversion follows the course of what is now Nuns Street and Kedleston Street and, if continued, would meet the Derwent near the former Great Northern Railway bridge. The river there is too deep to ford and the crossing must have been made via a new bridge. As there is no trace of such a structure, the bridge is assumed to have been of timber construction; in the Roman period these were not uncommon. On the eastern bank the course of the road can be traced northwards towards Breadsall *(Fig 4)*.

At the turn of the century, the evidence, although tenuous, suggests that Strutt's Park was dismantled rather than destroyed. The latest coin found in the fort area is one of the Emperor Domitian and can be dated to AD95-6. Unstratified early second-century pottery has alas been found which indicates

Figure 4. *Map showing second-century road system.*

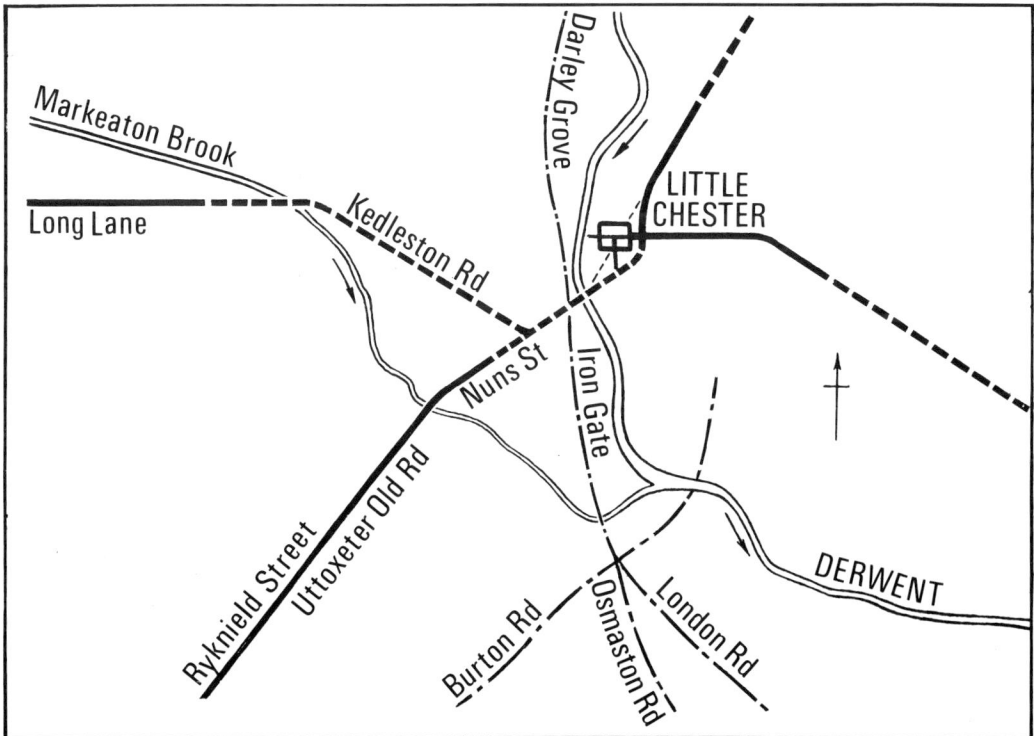

15

that the Strutt's Park fort possibly continued into the early years of the second century before being dismantled. Recent excavations at Chesterfield indicate that the fort there was dismantled at this time. It is not known for certain whether a new fort was then built on the low ground opposite at Little Chester, but as the garrison of Britain was being reduced at the time it does not seem likely.

THE SECOND CENTURY

IN the early years of the second century under the Emperor Trajan, the Roman Empire on the Continent reached its greatest extent; only in Britain did it decrease. The withdrawal of a legion by Domitian and of auxiliary troops by Trajan resulted in the loss of Agricola's conquests in Scotland. Insufficient troops to man the extended frontiers resulted in insurrections throughout the empire and at the end of Trajan's reign in AD117 there was much loss of life in Britain. At this time the Ninth Legion was engaged in heavy fighting with the Caledonians and soon afterwards disappears from history, its base at York being taken over by the Sixth Legion.

Trajan's successor, Hadrian, adopted a policy of containment. He realized the need to put the administration of the empire on a firm footing and to that end spent many years of his reign (AD117-138) touring the provinces instituting reforms. One of his first visits was to war-torn Britain, where he found many things that needed his attention. Unlike previous emperors, who would have ordered an expedition into Caledonia to recover the province, he directed that a stone wall be built across the country from the Tyne to the Solway 'to separate the Romans from the barbarians'.

Hadrian was the first emperor to do such a thing. He was a man of immense energy, disdaining to ride. It was his custom to march beside his troops. At the end of a long day he would sit with them on the ground and share their plain fare: cornmeal biscuits washed down with bitter wine.

On his tour through the province, Hadrian may have investigated the lead industry and found the sub-contracting arrangements unsatisfactory. There exists an ingot of lead inscribed IMP CAES HADRIANI AVG MET LVT, which may well imply that imperial control was reimposed. At this time the military supervision of the Brigantes was relaxed and many forts in the Pennines were dismantled.

What effect this new policy had at Little Chester is unclear. Although a new fort may not have been built on the eastern bank of the river to replace that on Strutt's Park, the site was certainly occupied and had been since the first century. The large stone buildings on the site of the Manor House Farm and to the north in the nursery gardens were in use for many years and may date from the time of Hadrian; certainly large amounts of samian pottery (the high-grade pottery used by officers) dating from this period have been found in the vicinity.

Upon the death of Hadrian in AD138, Antoninus Pius succeeded as emperor. In contrast to former emperors he endeavoured to govern with a bias towards the public well-being, rather than towards personal glory.

The Greek historian Pausanias wrote: 'Antoninus Pius never willingly made war: but when the Moors took up arms against Rome he drove them off their land . . . he also deprived the Brigantes in Britain of the greater part of their territory because they too had become aggressive and attacked the district of Genunia, whose inhabitants were subject to Rome.' This statement has been disbelieved by some modern historians, who point out that Brigantian lands for many years had lain within the boundaries of the empire and that the first act of this 'peaceful' emperor was to order the reoccupation of Lowland Scotland, the construction of a second wall, and the building of a series of forts across the country from the Forth to the Clyde. If, however, it is accepted that Pausanias is correct, it must also be accepted that Brigantia continued as an autonomous state until the middle of the second century. How this came about is suggested opposite.

It has been established by excavation that during the reign of Hadrian many forts were abandoned in Brigantian territory. It is unlikely that Hadrian would have ordered this to be done if the Brigantes had been the cause of the trouble in the early years of his reign.

At this time, marauding Caledonians were devastating the north and the Brigantes must have taken the brunt of the inevitable looting. In defending themselves they probably stabilized the situation by confining the trouble to the north. As a reward for what appeared to be loyalty, Hadrian may well have reinstated the privilege of self-rule.

This arrangement, often made in the early years of the empire, did not normally outlast the lifetime of the current native ruler. Upon his demise the Roman rule was usually re-established. During the reign of Antoninus Pius the policy of absorption was probably well advanced in the more prosperous parts of Brigantia. However, the Brigantian chiefs probably assumed that Genunia was still part of their tribal lands over which they had every right to assert their authority. The Romans, however, regarded the incident as a Brigantian insurrection and an attack on people now subject to Rome. The garrison on the Northern Antonine Wall was temporarily withdrawn to confront them and the tribe was subsequently humbled and deprived of the greater part of its land.

THE FORT AT LITTLE CHESTER

IT WAS thought that evidence of a Brigantian insurrection in AD154 had been found at Little Chester. The floor of the building which lies beneath the clay rampart in the nursery garden was found on excavation to be covered by a layer of ash. To the south, at the south-east corner of the fort, on the site of the former railway embankment, wooden buildings of this period were revealed which had been burnt with their contents. The burnt remains on both these sites were overlain by a fort rampart composed of slabs of clay placed directly on top of the ashes. *[Fig 11.A & K]*

This clearly indicates that after its destruction by fire, the site was immediately occupied by the military and defences constructed in some haste. Examination of some samian pottery discovered sealed beneath the clay rampart at the south-east corner of the fort revealed that they were the products of the potter Paternus, who started working around AD160, some six or seven years after the presumed Brigantian revolt.

The defences of the fort *[Fig 13]* were rectangular in plan, enclosing an area of approximately seven acres, which was surrounded by two deep ditches spaced 100ft apart. The defensive work consisted of a strong timber stockade forming the frontage of the clay rampart, the whole structure originally being some 15ft high by 20ft thick.

Ryknield Street, which made the crossing of the river via a wooden bridge, was now diverted around the new defences *[Fig 4]*. The masonry building that occupied the site of Manor House Farm was retained and incorporated within the defences. The eastern side of the building was partly buried in the clay rampart and was south of, and adjacent to, the newly-formed east gate of the fort *[Fig 11.E]*. North of Old Chester Road, in the nursery garden, a large Roman building has been partly uncovered (and is not to be confused with the dismantled structure underlying the clay rampart). To the west of this building a large amount of samian pottery was found.

The headquarters building *(principia)* occupied the central area, now the playing-field car-park, at the junction of City Road and Old Chester Road. Such a building normally consisted of a courtyard attached to a building which contained a large hall *(basilica)* and four administrative offices, two on either side of the Shrine of the Standards, where it was usual for a statue of the Emperor to stand.

From the shrine there was often a flight of stairs leading down to an underground strongroom where the pay chest of the garrison was kept. In addition to the headquarters building it can be assumed that other buildings

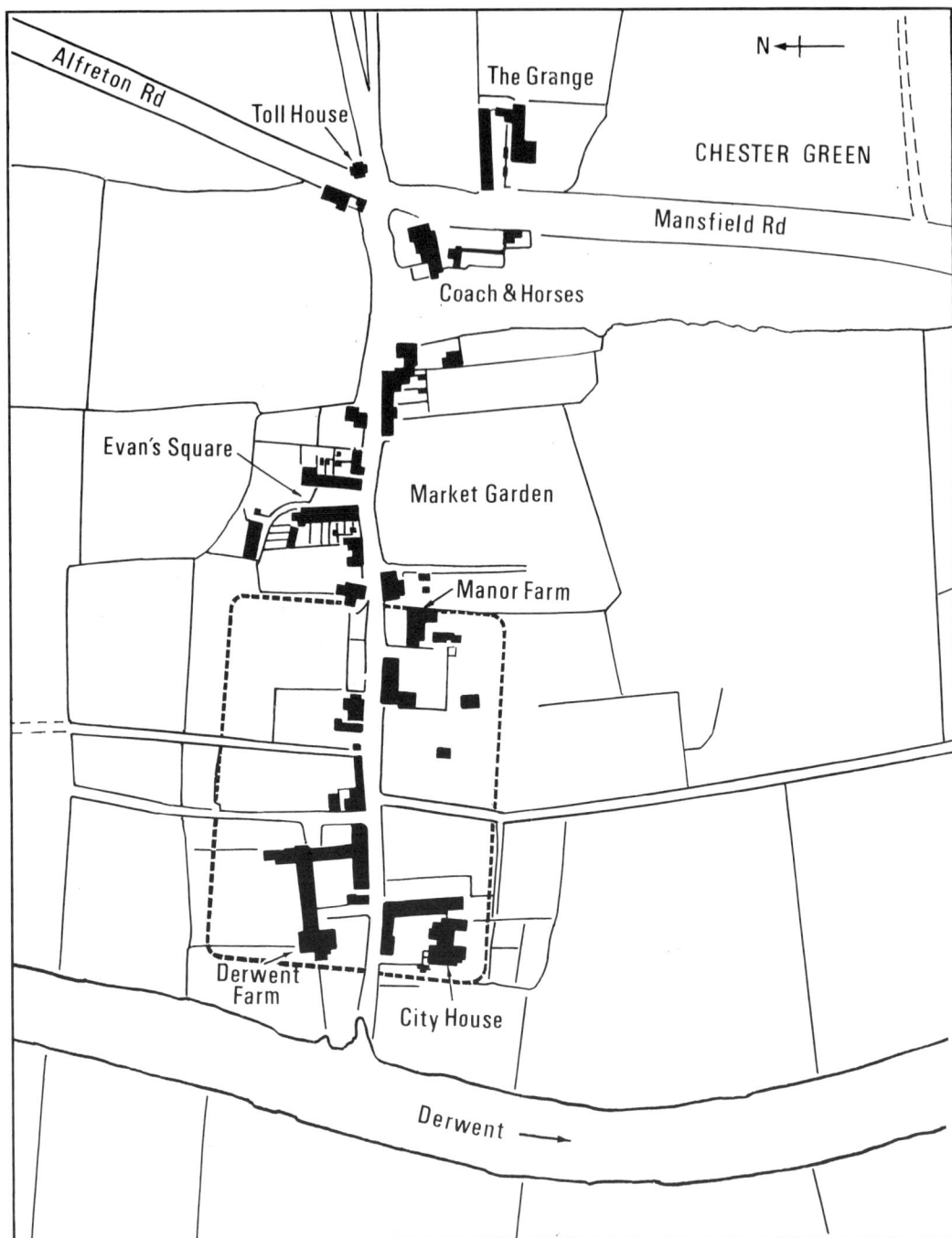

Figure 5. *Map of Little Chester, 1852.*

would be the commandant's house
(praetorium), granaries *(horrea)*, a hospital
(valetudinarium) and sometimes an armoury
workshop *(fabricae)*.

When the foundations for a block of flats
immediately to the east of the car-park were
cut in 1965, no remains were found likely to
be that of a *praetorium*. However, hearths and

charcoal deposits were uncovered, consistent with industrial working. It is therefore suggested that, at Little Chester, the armoury workshop lay to the east of the headquarters building and the commandant's house to the west. If this is the case, then the space remaining near the western rampart would be too small for the granaries and was probably filled by the hospital block.

The west gate was partially excavated in 1968. It was found that the road passing through it was composed of many layers, indicating that it was used over a long period of time. This road undoubtedly ran to the river where it was at one time believed there was a bridge. More likely it was the site of a wharf which served the fort.

THE GARRISON

NO inscriptions have yet been found at Little Chester. The only reference to the site from ancient sources is a late version of its name, Derbentione, which appears between Lutudarum and Salinae in a seventh-century list of towns *(The Ravenna Cosmography)*.

The names of the units which garrisoned the fort are unknown and the only hint of the type of unit originally stationed there is the size of the fort. As it covers an area of some seven acres and is amongst the largest of auxiliary forts, it must have been occupied by one of the larger auxiliary units. The biggest cavalry unit was the *ala milliaria* (a thousand horsemen), only one of which was stationed in Britain, and this appears to have occupied the 9.25 acre fort at Stanwix on Hadrian's Wall.

The only unit that appears suitable for Little Chester is a *cohors equitata milliaria,* which consisted of ten centuries of infantry, the same number as for a *cohors peditata milliaria,* but with the addition of 240 cavalry divided into four troops of 60 horsemen. There were five of these units stationed in Britain.

Cohors I Vangionum Milliaria Equitata
Cohors II Tungrorum Milliaria Equitata

Cohors I Fida Vardullorum Milliaria Equitata
Cohors I Aelia Hispanorum Milliaria Equitata
Cohors I Nervana Germanorum Milliaria Equitata

In the late second century, a detachment of the *I Vangionum* was stationed at Benwell on Hadrian's Wall. The *I Nervana* followed by the *II Tungrorum* are recorded at Birrens in Scotland and the *Fida Vardullorum* at Corbridge and Lanchester. Which of the above units initially garrisoned Little Chester must be left to conjecture.

The only reference to a Roman unit in Derbyshire, the first cohort of Aquitanians, is recorded on an inscription found in the principia of the Roman fort at Brough-on-Noe dated to the period AD154-8. This cohort is also mentioned on an altar which was found in the grounds of Haddon hall near Bakewell.

THE CIVIL SETTLEMENT

THE large number of troops stationed at Little Chester encouraged civilian development along the roads adjacent to the fort. Evidence of this was obtained by Charles Sherwin in 1926, when he entirely uncovered Ryknield Street north of the fort for a quarter of a mile and trenched on either side of it *(Plate7)*. Alongside the road he discovered the remains of buildings of *'a humble kind, devoid of architectural features'*.

Completely clearing the site of one building which was more substantial than the others, he found that the stones forming the threshold had been recessed to accommodate shutters. Also, set into the floor were a number of well-worn mill stones, which suggests that the building was once a baker's shop *(Plate 3)*.

The industrial suburb lay alongside the road running eastwards from the fort. On the Racecourse Playing Fields, where this road turns towards Sawley, evidence of industrial working has been found. Numerous remains of ovens and furnaces used in the making of iron and bronze articles have been uncovered. Further east lay pottery kilns, eighteen of which have so far been excavated.

Plate 1. *House footings (above) built over the foundations of a substantial Roman building on the site of Manor Farm, Pickford's. Despite being a site of national importance, permission was given for the Roman buildings and defensive wall to be destroyed.*

Plate 2. *Roman building destroyed 5 August 1987.*

Above: Plate 3. *The baker's shop and Ryknield Street, 1926.*

Below: Plate 4. *The south wall of the Roman fort, 1926.*

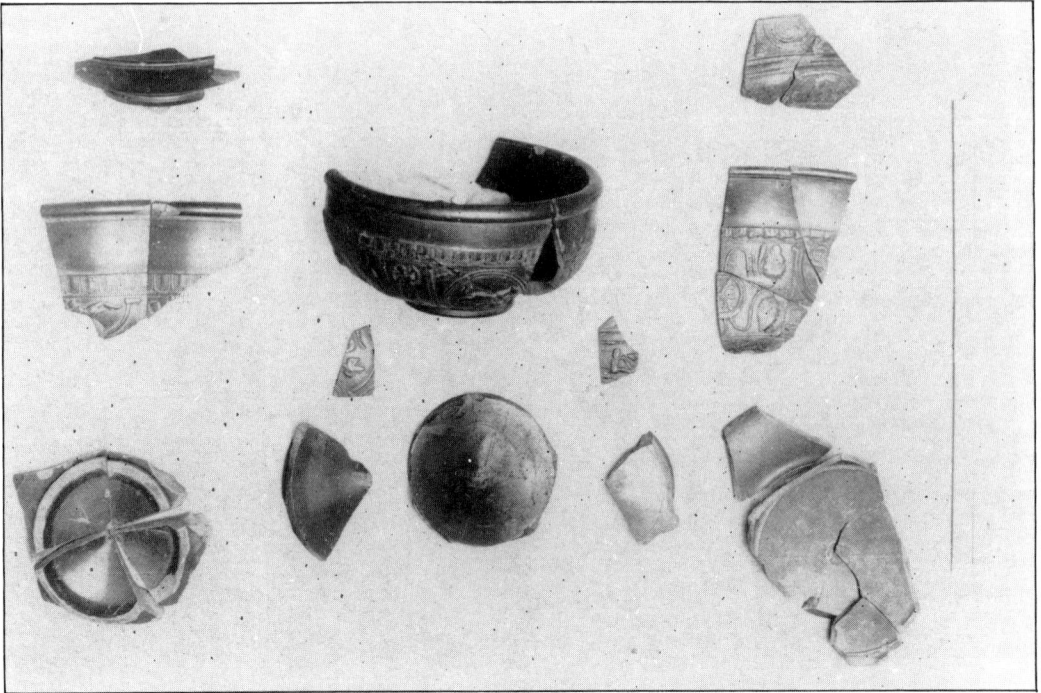

Above: Plate 5. *Samian Pottery from the civil settlement alongside Ryknield Street, 1926. Below:* Plate 6. *Coarse pottery from the civil settlement alongside Ryknield Street, 1926.*

Above: Plate 7. *Ryknield Street uncovered for a quarter of a mile in 1926.* *Below:* Plate 8. *Eastern wall of fort destroyed 1988 (see Figure 11.K).*

THE EXCAVATIONS AT
LITTLE CHESTER 1926.

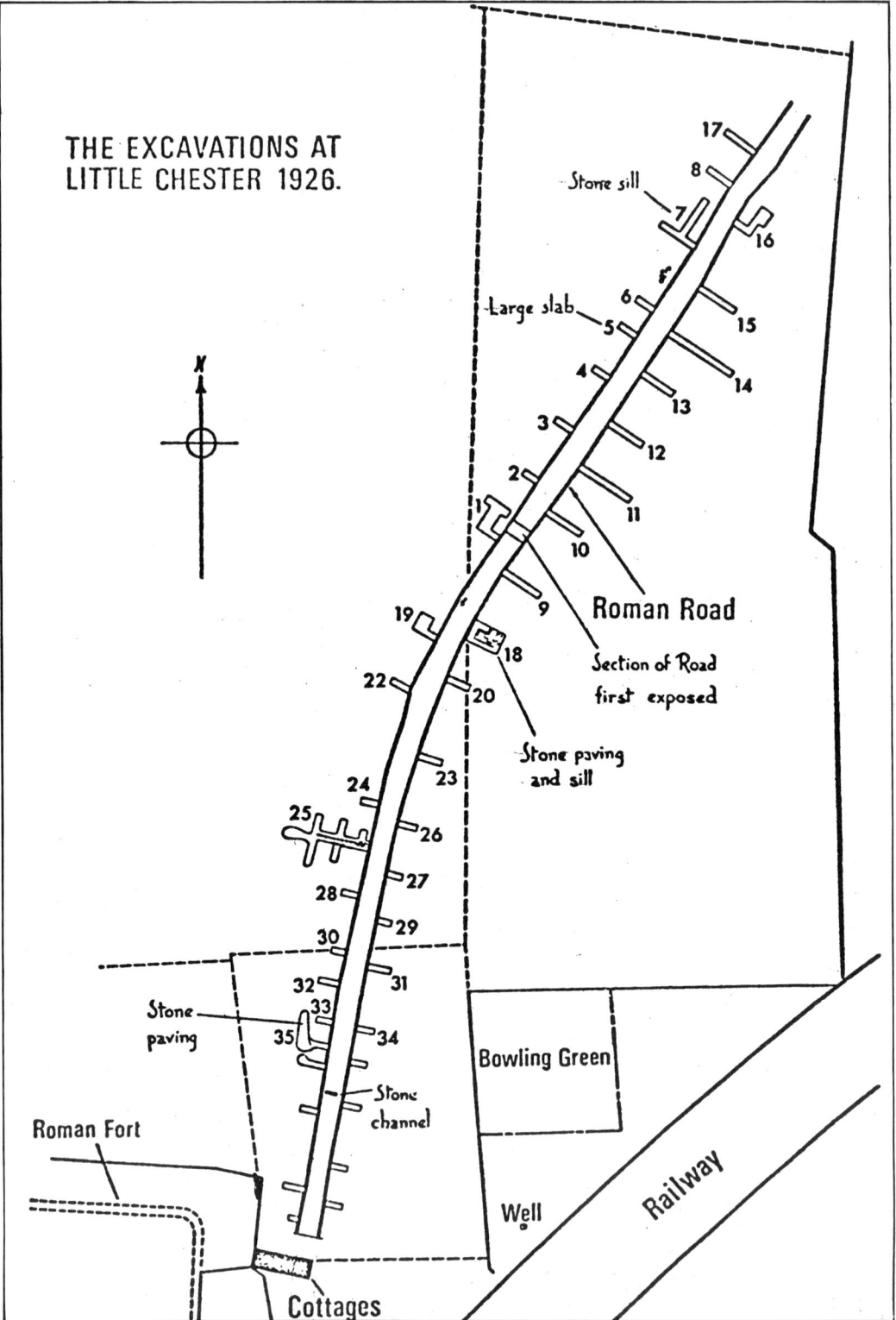

Stone sill

Large slab

Roman Road

Section of Road
first exposed

Stone paving
and sill

Stone paving

Stone
channel

Roman Fort

Bowling Green

Well

Railway

Cottages

When the settlement grew in size it would have been granted the legal status of a *vicus* and allowed to manage its own parochial affairs subject always to the agreement of the commandant.

The Midland Railway lies between Little Chester and the Roman industrial suburb. On 19 September 1861, whilst digging the foundations of a corn shed for the railway company, workmen recovered samian pottery at a depth of 13ft embedded in soft black mud lying upon gravel. At the time of discovery it was assumed that these sherds were lying in a former bed of the Derwent. They were, however, more likely to have been lying in a defensive ditch. This may have been connected with the civil settlement, or could possibly have belonged to a satellite fort or a predecessor to the main fort.

LOCAL POTTERY

POTTERS did not rank highly on the social scale and were confined to the edges of settlements, with their kilns sited so that the prevailing wind took the smoke away from the residential area.

Pottery manufacture *(Fig 15)* began in Derby in the first century, no doubt to supply the fort then situated on Strutt's Park. Some of these first-century products were neatly made but many were thick and clumsy, suggesting native work. A typical kiln consisted of a stokehole with a flue leading to a subterranean furnace chamber of baked clay, usually circular in plan, above which was an oven in which the pottery was fired.

By the end of the first century the kilns were all of this type *(Fig 16)*. They produced jars, bowls and dishes in large quantities. Itinerant potters also used the site and *Septiminus, Aesticus* and *Primus* were potters who stamped their names on the rims of mortaria. Mortaria

Figure 6. *(opposite): Map showing the excavation of Ryknield Street.*

were spouted bowls with grit embedded in the inner surface and were used for mixing herbs. The manufacture of pottery ceased in the mid-second century, when the potters apparently moved on to the Hazelwood-Holbrook area and began mass production of the wide-mouthed storage jars now known as Derbyshire ware.

This pottery is easily recognized as it has a distinctive hard pimply surface resembling 'petrified goose flesh'. These jars were produced in three sizes (small, medium and large), possibly as utilitarian containers for beans grown in southern Derbyshire. The degree of standardization suggests a military contract. The distribution also supports this theory, as few examples are found south of the Trent. *(Plate 23)*

SAMIAN POTTERY

ONE product that the London merchants imported into the country from France in great quantity was samian pottery. This ware was produced in a variety of standard shapes. It is bright red in colour and has a smooth glossy surface. It was favoured by the well-to-do and a surprising amount has been found at Little Chester *(Fig 19.B)*.

The potters frequently stamped their names on their products and many bowls have distinctive decorations (from a study of which it is possible to deduce the date of bowls with great accuracy, *Fig 20*). Scenes from classical mythology are depicted. These include Venus, the goddess of Love, Bacchus the god of Wine, satyrs and dancing girls. The military market was catered for with figures of Victory, Hercules, gladiatorial conflicts, trophies and captives. It would seem that the artistic taste of the fighting man has not greatly changed through the ages.

If ever a samian vessel came into the possession of a member of the general public, it was highly prized. Broken bowls have been found at Little Chester pieced together and held in place with lead rivets.

Above: Plate 9. *From left to right: John Potts, Roger Salt, Nigel Brassington and Michael Bond excavating on the Racecourse Playing Fields, 1968. Below:* Plate 10. *A tray of finds.*

Above: Plate 11. *Racecourse Playing Fields, Kiln 3, 1968. Below:* Plate 12. *Racecourse Playing Fields, Kiln 4a, 1972.*

Above: Plate 13. *Racecourse Playing Fields, 1968. On the left two small 'experimental' kilns; on the right the well-preserved Kiln 1b.* Below: Plate 14. *Racecourse Playing Fields, Kiln 2b, 1968.*

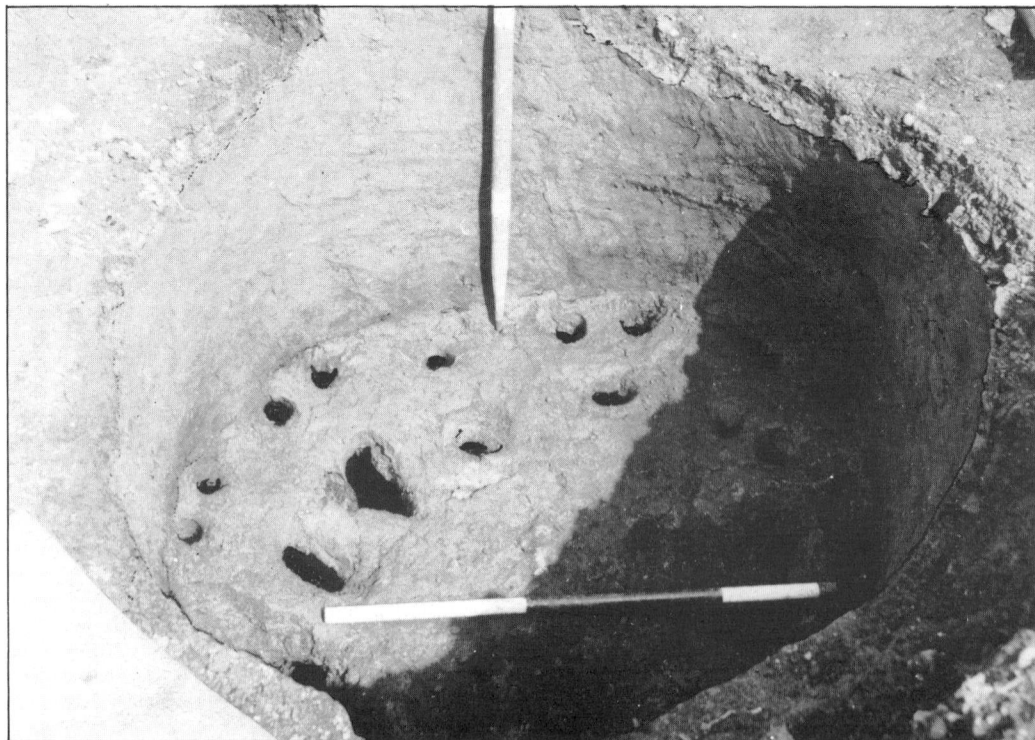

Top left: Plate 16. *Industrial oven.* Plate 17. *Bottom left: Vandalized kiln.* Plate 18. *Right: Kiln 2c, 1968.*

Plate 18.: *Hazelwood. Kiln 2, Lumb brook, 1972. This produced Derbyshire Ware.*

Above: Plate 19. *Stone wall and clay rampart on the Pickford's site (see* Figure 11.E). *Below:* Figure 7. *Pottery found near the east gate.*

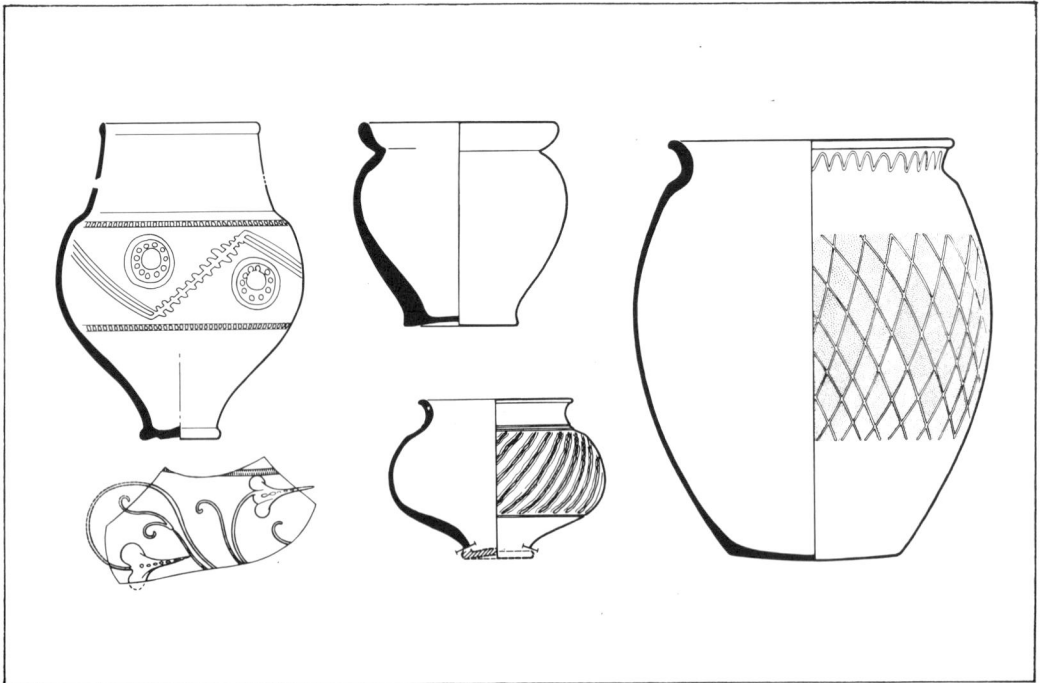

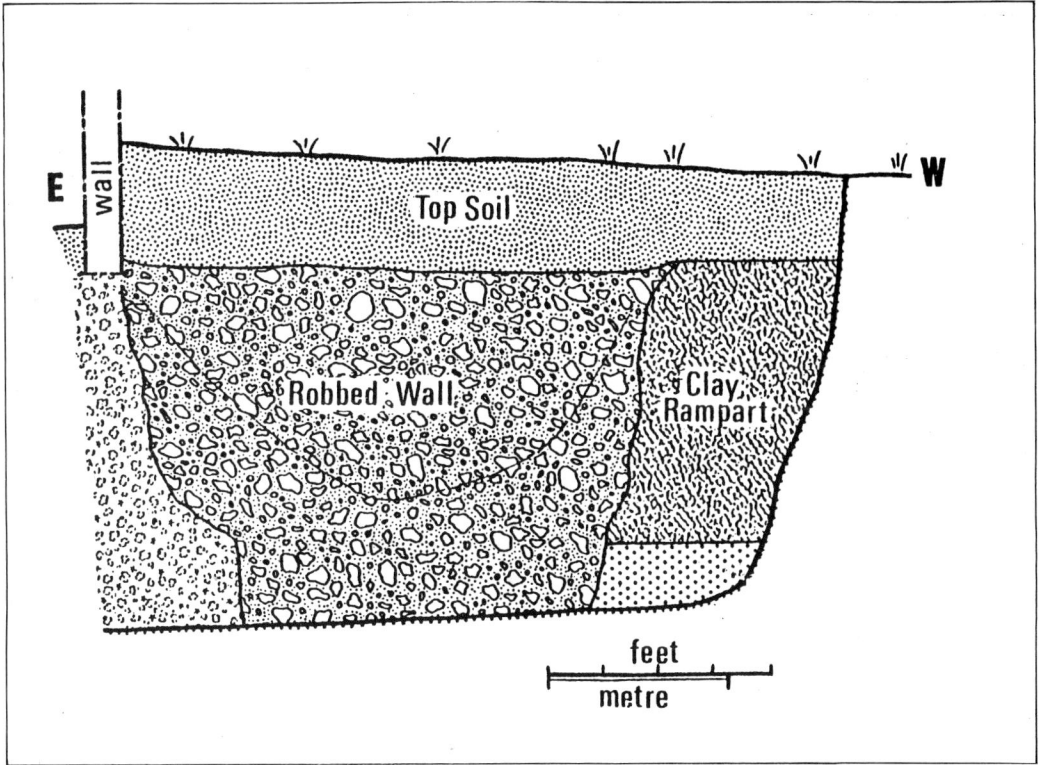

Above: Figure 8. *Section through the robbed defensive wall (see* Figure 11.B*) Below:* Figure 9. *Section through the eastern wall and rampart (see* Figure 11.A*).*

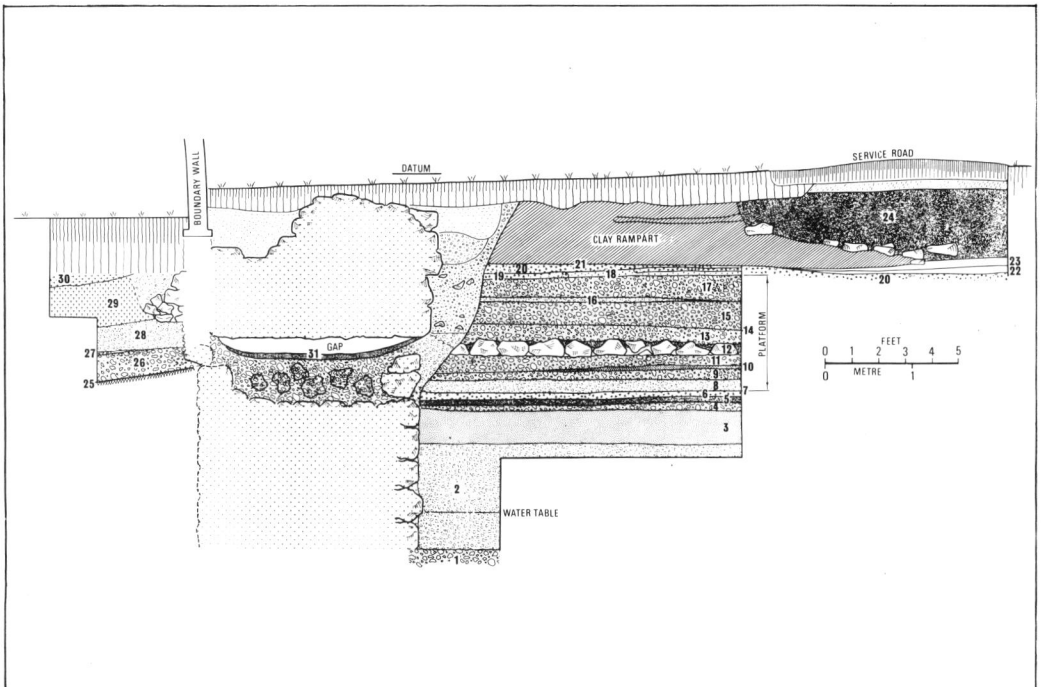

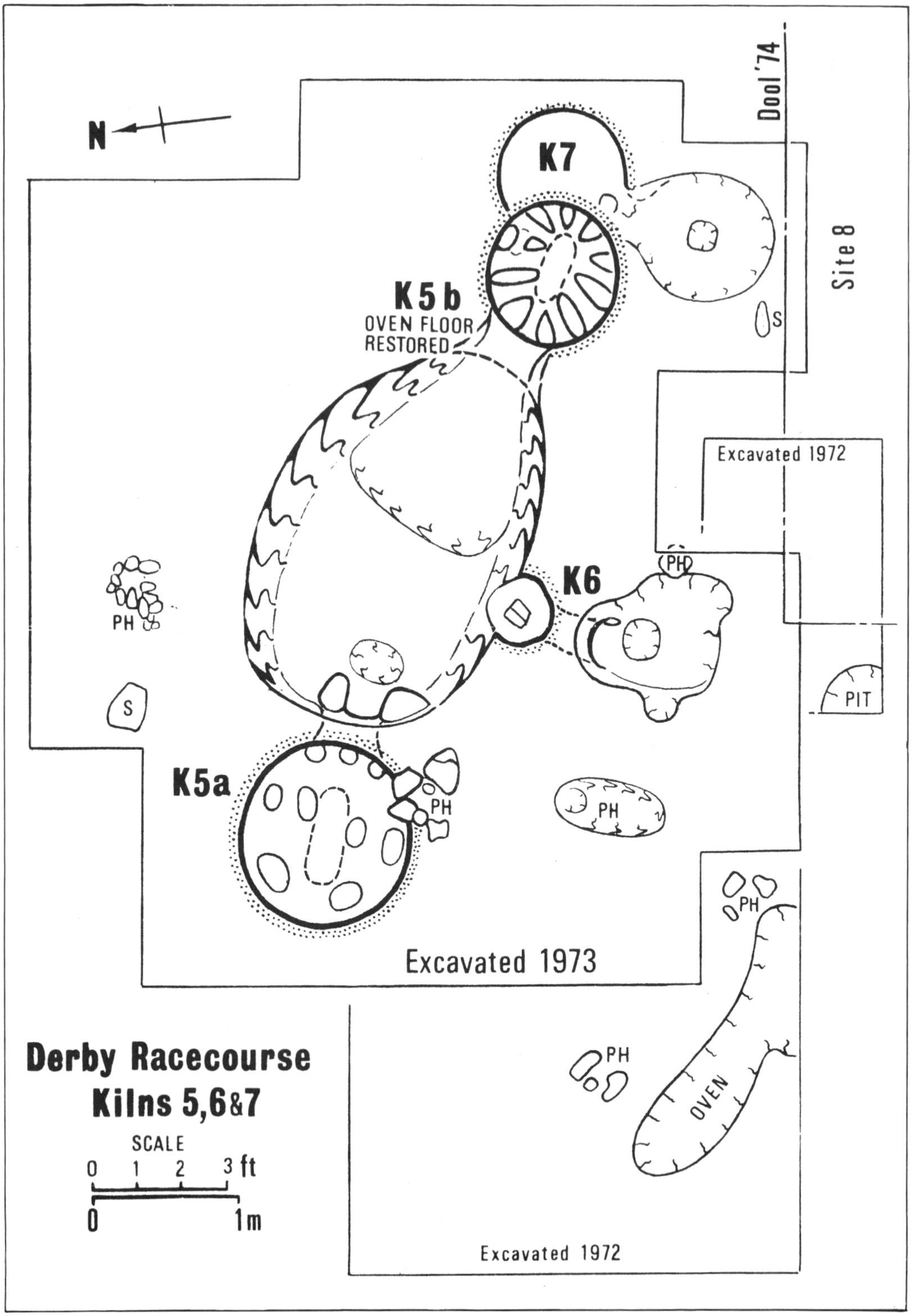

N

K7

K5b
OVEN FLOOR
RESTORED

K6

PH

S

K5a

PH

PH

Dool '74

Site 8

Excavated 1972

PH

PIT

PH

Excavated 1973

PH

PH

OVEN

**Derby Racecourse
Kilns 5,6&7**

SCALE
0 1 2 3 ft

0   1m

Excavated 1972

Figure 10. *A kiln group on the Derby Racecourse Playing Fields.*

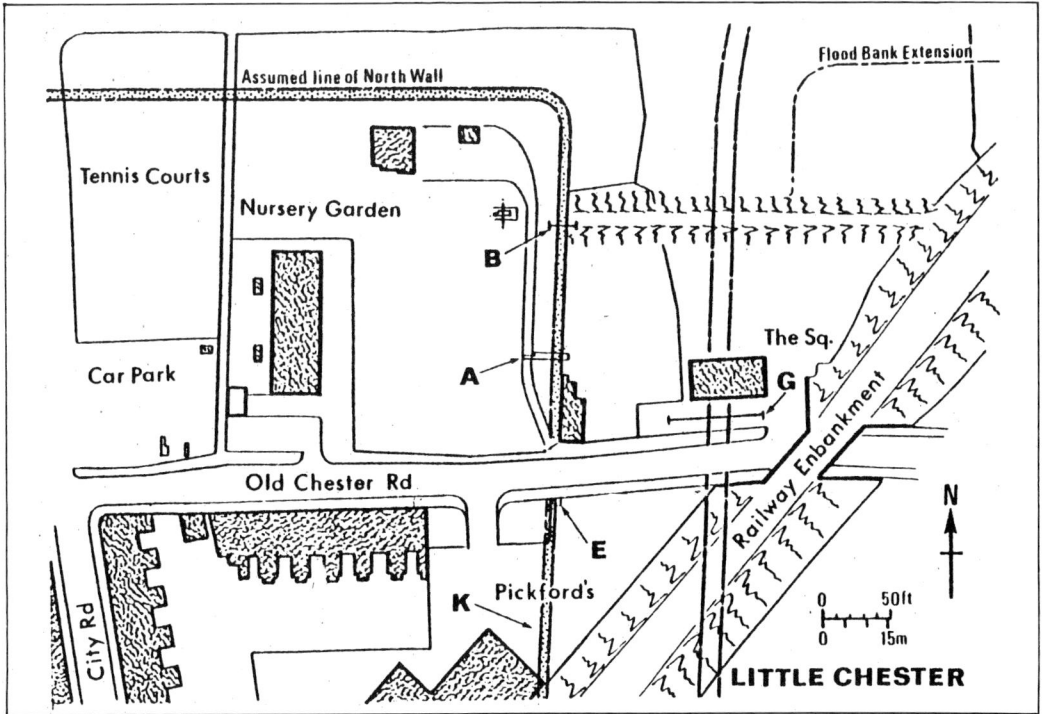

Figure 11. Map showing the archaeological site at Little Chester.

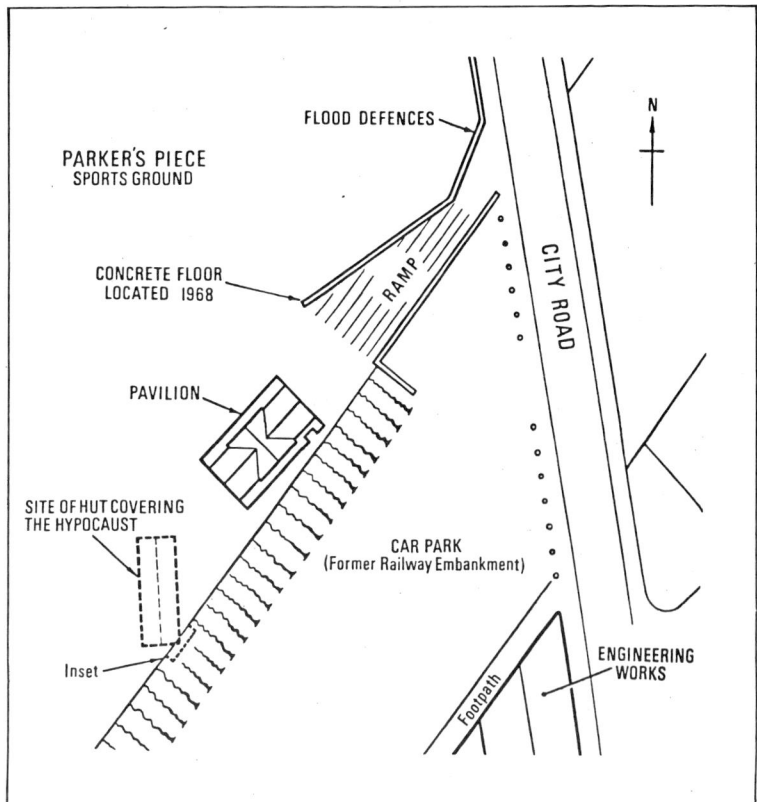

Figure 12. Map of Parker's Piece, the former Derby School playing fields, at Little Chester.

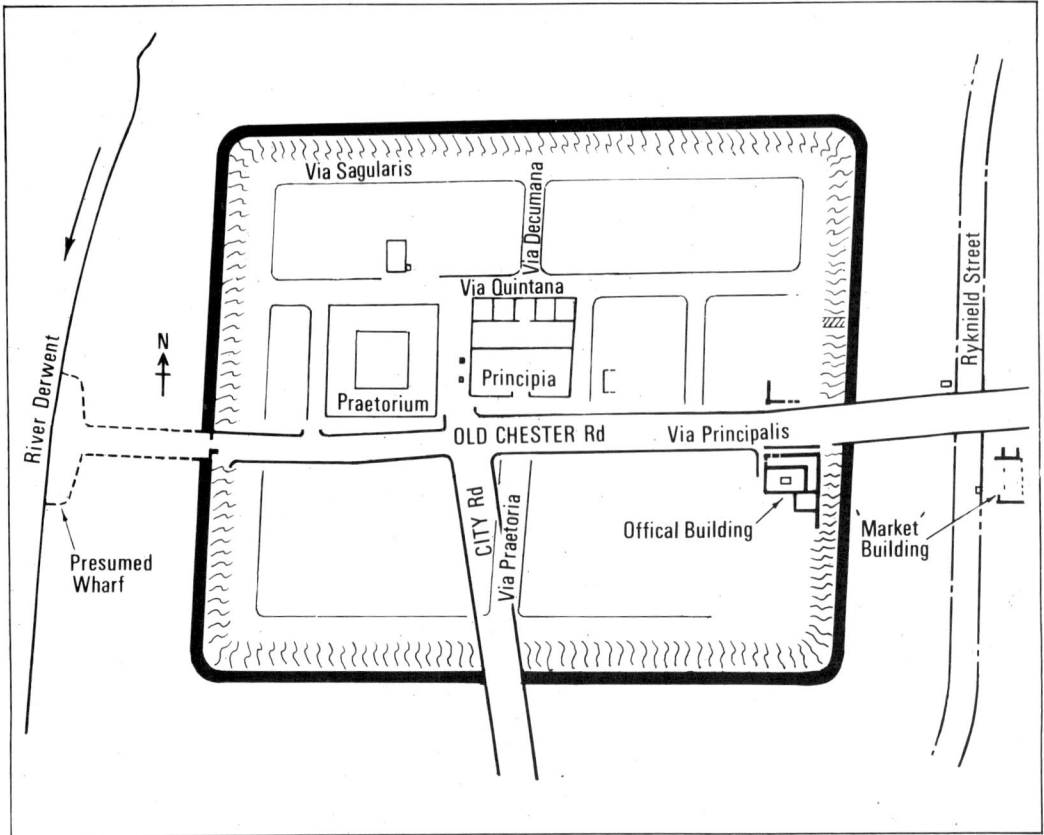

Figure 13. *Plan of the second-century fort at Little Chester.*

OTHER TRADES

THE army used vast quantities of leather, therefore drovers, slaughterers, butchers, tanners and leather workers would be required. The need for metal would necessitate smelters and smiths for both iron and bronze. Wood was wanted for both buildings and fuel, hence there would be carpenters and sawyers. All these trades would need the services of carters and porters. Women, for the most part, would be engaged in domestic spinning and weaving.

The tradesmen and their families, whose livelihood depended on their ability to supply the basic needs of the garrison, lived either in or close by their workshops. The emphasis for them was on work and not pleasure. Tethered in every convenient and inconvenient spot would be sheep and the occasional goat. Sheep were kept not only for their wool but also for dairying, ewes' milk being required for cheese. In the baker's shop, a pig, regarded as a family pet, would be found eating the miller's waste bran. The stench of animals was ever-present and spilt feed made mice a serious pest. Dormice, their larger edible cousins, were, however, imported from the Continent, kept in cages or ceramic jars and fattened for the table. They were considered a great delicacy when stuffed with minced pork. The presence of ducks, geese, cats and dogs can also be taken for granted. The young women of the settlement would cover themselves with perfume in an attempt to mask the resultant vile smell and many fragments of their perfume flasks have been found *[Fig 14]*.

Any young officer forced to stay the night in such a rural backwater would no doubt find

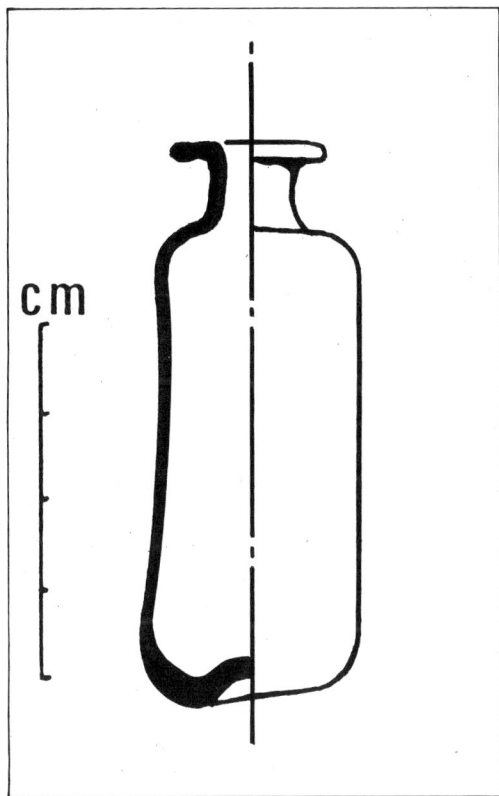

cm

Figure 14. *Green glass perfume flask.*

the tenor of provincial life tedious in the extreme and yearn for the delights of civilized society, especially that of Rome, where Horace tells us the streets were crowded with *'flute-girls, drug pushers, beggars, actresses and buffoons'*.

Workmen, who lived in the overcrowded tenements of the capital, were unable to compete with the cheap goods, products of slave labour, which flooded in from the empire. To avoid trouble, the government subsidized them with free food, with the result that thousands lived on this dole and did no work. They spent their time betting on the results of chariot races and gladiatorial fights in the arena.

Things would have been very different at Little Chester, as no subsidy was paid and everyone and everything was taxed. There was little relief from monotonous toil, but from

time to time a showman would arrive with a troop of gladiators, singers and dancers to entertain the garrison.

GRAFFITI AND FREE SPEECH

AS the knowledge of Latin and Roman customs spread to the provinces, even humble workmen learnt to read and write. Lacking our modern paper they wrote on whatever would serve the purpose, for example potsherds and wood shavings. A potsherd of Italian red ware found at Leicester had been used as an amulet and had the following inscription neatly scratched upon it:

> VERECVNDA
> LVDIA LVC
> IVS GLA DIA
> TOR

Evidently a girl known, doubtless inappropriately, as Verecunda (Modesty) had linked her name with that of Lucius, a star of the gladiatorial arena.

Above the doorways of their shops craftsmen would paint signs to encourage custom which promised careful work and service. An inn sign would have a picture showing people drinking. Scratched on every available wall would be a mass of graffiti, the literary products of the inhabitants. Examples from Herculaneum and Pompeii, preserved when those cities were buried in volcanic ash, give some indication of what might have been written on walls at Little Chester. There were the young lovers:

> *'Portumnous loves Amphianda,*
> *Januarius loves Veneria.*
> *We pray to you, O Venus,*
> *That you will remember us,*
> *This only we ask of you'.*

Also the clumsy suitor:

> *'Alexander salutes Livia and*
> *states that he is in good health'.*

Livia's reply to the ham-handed approach would doubtless have the approval of the

35

modern miss; it seems that some things never change:

> 'What is it to me whether your
> health is good or bad.
> You can drop dead tomorrow
> for all I care'.

The messages written on the ale house walls were often uncomplimentary in the extreme:

> 'May you innkeeper to a demon,
> die drowned in your own uric-wine.
> Keeping the best for yourself,
> you sell us the dross you swine.'

This, and much worse, must have had its counterpart at Little Chester. It well illustrates that the Romans retained the coarse outspokeness of the peasant, despite their rigid class structure. No one was immune from scurrilous attacks, not even the emperor (Nero being referred to as 'that drunken wine-flushed sot'). Remarks were pitiless and brutally frank. People were known by their deformities, nicknames such as 'bandy-legs' or 'one-eye' quickly became the family name of the afflicted. It was known that Julius Caesar had a weakness for pretty women and that he was very conscious of going bald. During his triumphal procession through Rome the soldiers behind his chariot began to chant:

'Romans, Romans, lock up your wives,
we bring the bald-headed adulterer'.

It was the custom, not even the anger of Caesar could silence them.

COMMERCE

GOOD communications are essential for commerce and the metalled roads that crossed the country made the transport of goods both swift and easy. Among the items sold in bulk at Little Chester were shellfish, olive oil and wine. Many fragments of amphorae have been found that would have carried fish, fruit, oil and perfumes from Seville, and wine from Provence. A sherd from a globular amphora found in 1979 carried the graffito: 'In the consulship of Macrinus and Celsus, the work of . . .vatus.' This can be dated to the year AD164.

Merchants communicated with one another by private post. Messages scratched on beeswax were dispatched, sealed within small flat wooden boxes similar in size to cigarette cases. After being read by the recipients, the messages were erased by smoothing the surface and a reply written (Fig 19.A). One of these cases containing a message from a merchant to his servant has been found in London. It read:

> 'From Rufus, son of Callisunus. Greetings
> to you Epillicus and all your companions.
> I believe you have heard that I am well.
> If you have made an inventory please
> send it to me. Look after everything
> carefully and see to it that you turn that
> slave-girl into cash. . .'

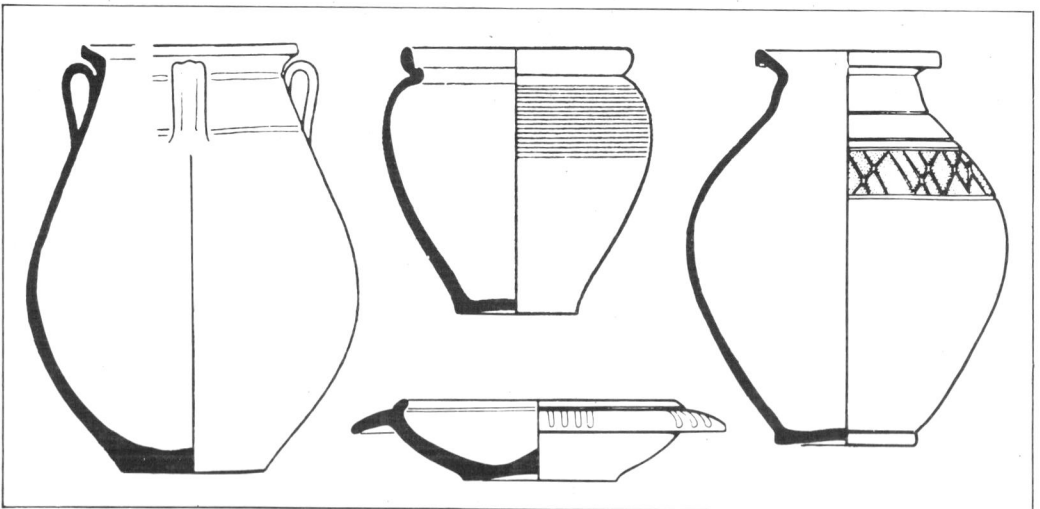

Figure 15. Local products.

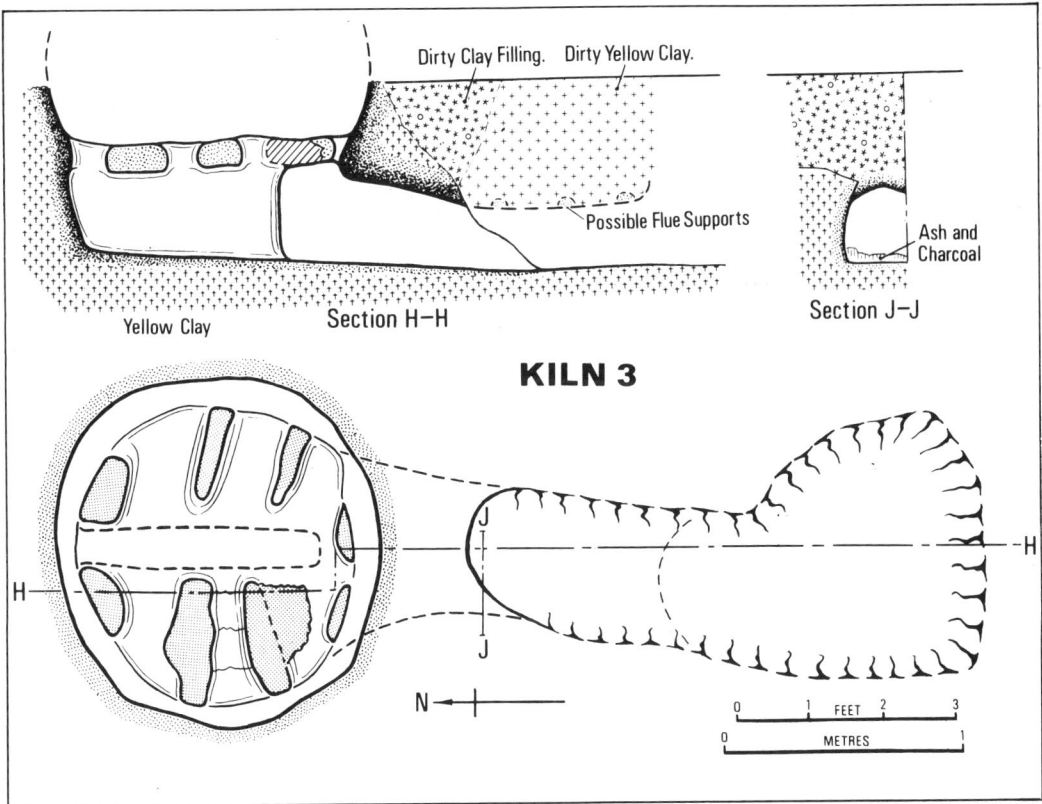

Figure 16. *Early second-century pottery kiln, Derby Racecourse Playing Fields.*

HEALTH

THE Life expectancy of the common people was a little over forty years. Over a fifth of the population were dead before the age of twenty. Only half of the survivors lived beyond the age of twenty-five and these all showed some sign of degenerative diseases of the spine. However, there was little dental decay, and it is known from other sites that many of the more well-to-do cleaned their teeth with a mixture of charcoal and crushed oyster shells. The average height of the men was 5ft 7in (1.70m), and 5ft 2in (1.59m) for the women.

Contagious diseases such as anthrax, tuberculosis, typhus, dysentery, smallpox and tetanus, would from time to time rage through the settlement and take a heavy toll of the inhabitants. Many were doubtless also killed by 'home remedies'. The Romans had many vile concoctions containing curious ingredients such as gladiator's blood or child's brains. The smoke of roasted cow dung inhaled through a reed was thought to be beneficial; it was the nearest they came to smoking.

THE CEMETERY

A BURIAL ground was discovered in November 1978 by bulldozers removing the banking of a former hedgerow on the Racecourse Playing Fields. It quickly became apparent that here was the eastern boundary of the settlement, for Roman law stated that no burials, other than infants, could take place within the limits of the town.

The Roman road leading to Sawley was exposed and on the northern side lay the

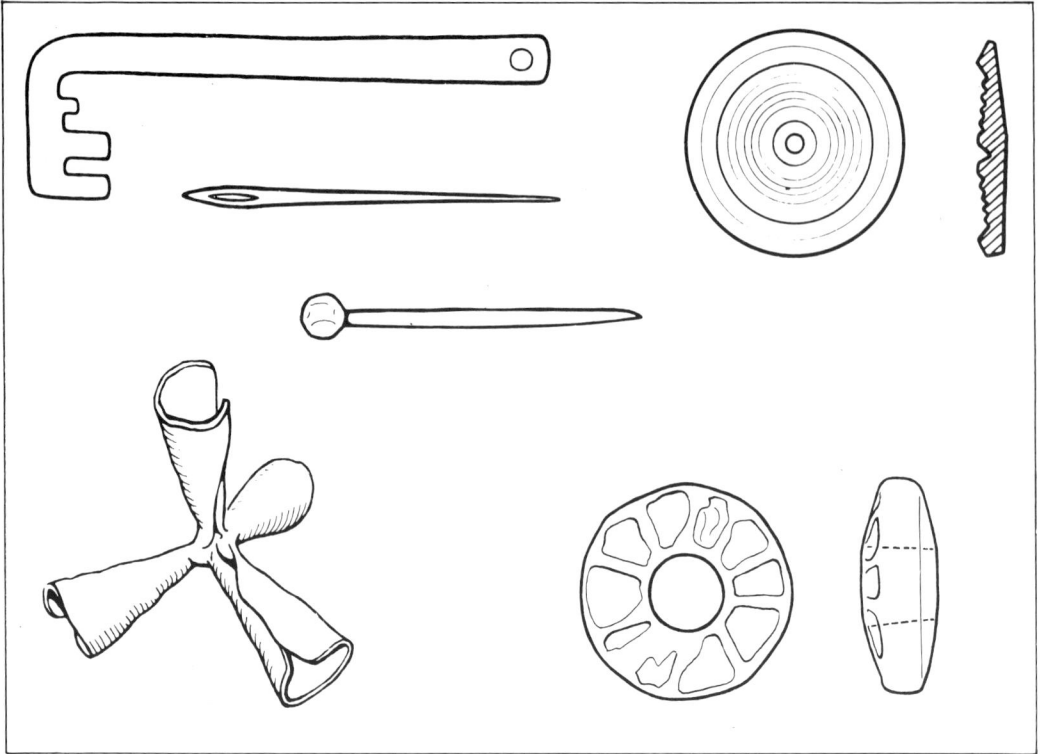

Figure 17. *House key, bronze needle, bone pin, gaming counter, iron candle holder and lead spindle whorl.*

remains of five wayside tombs. These were examined and in one were found two cremation urns surrounded by ten votice lamps and the cremated remains of a pig. The significance of a cremated pig, which was found associated with many burials, is made clear by a remark of Cicero: *'Burials do not really become graves until the proper rites are performed and a pig slain.'*

Close by these mausolea, a large jug containing a cremation was found with a flagon placed above it as a stopper. In this type of burial a two-handled wine jar (amphora) was often used, buried with only the neck protruding above ground. The bereaved, when visiting the grave, would bring an offering of wine which was poured down to the remains of the deceased.

Some 65ft to the north lay a walled cemetery enclosing an area of 1,600 sq ft and containing both cremations and inhumations. A number of the inhumations were mutilated, the left hand

of one had been severed and other had been decapitated, some of these having the head placed between the knees. Two were buried face down. The reason for these mutilations is not clear, possibly it was a macabre rite to prevent the dead walking.

In the area between the enclosure and the wayside tombs lay three male burials which are thought to be military and have been dated to the early Antonine period. The first man had presumably died in bed; this is deduced from the fact that his cloak and sword belt *[Fig 21.A]* had been laid on top of him and his boots placed beside his feet. The second man was buried wrapped in his cloak. The third, a young man, still carried his knife and also had two coins, presumably the payment to Charon whose duty it was to ferry the soul over the black waters of the River Styx on its journey to the underworld.

The tombstones marking these burials are unfortunately missing, probably removed by

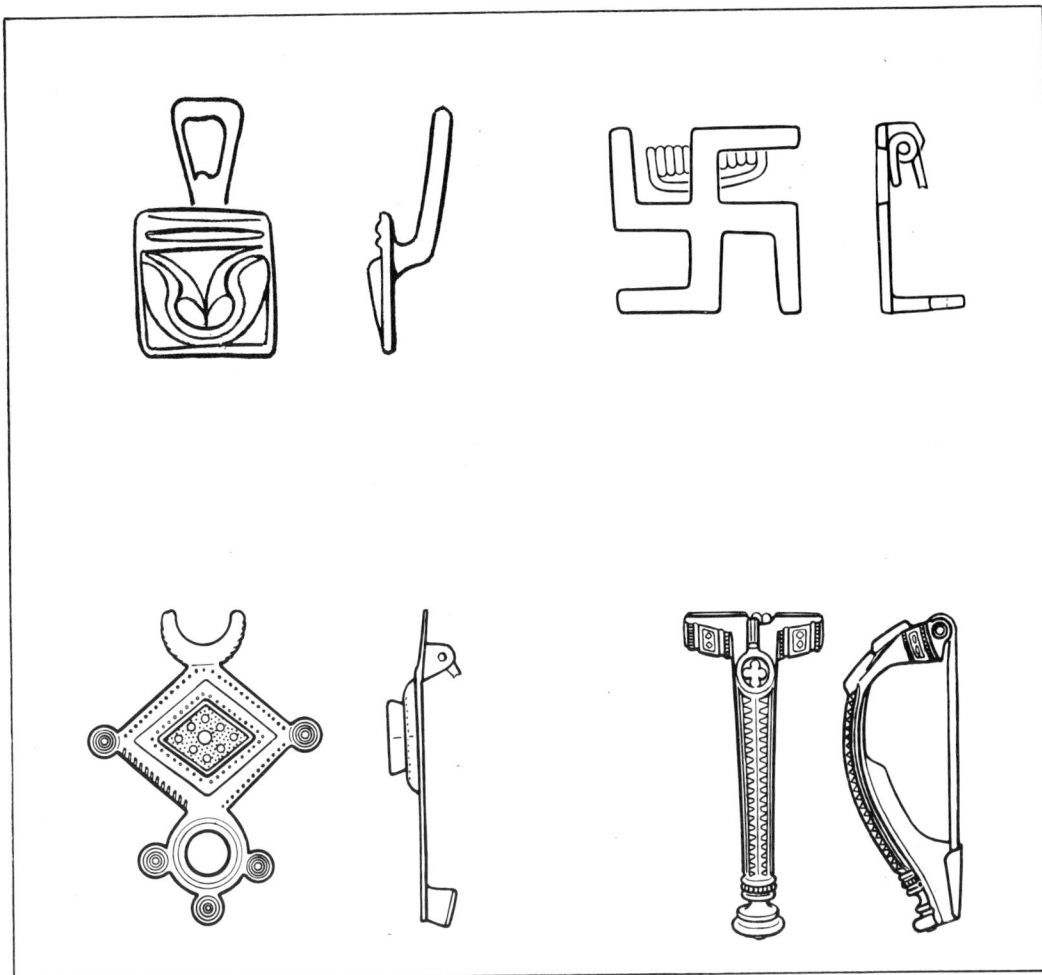

Figure 18. *Clock button and bronze brooches.*

stone robbers or cultivators. The epitaph of a soldier usually stated his name, rank, unit and length of service, information which is of great interest to archaeologists. Other inscriptions would have recorded personal grief, the loss of a wife or child. A soldier at York buried his infant daughter in an expensive stone coffin and had the following lines cut:

IN THE HANDS OF THE GODS
SIMPLICIA FLORENTINA
A MOST INNOCENT LITTLE THING
WHO LIVED TEN MONTHS
FELICIUS SIMPLEX, HER FATHER
A CENTURION OF THE
SIXTH LEGION HAD THIS
MEMORIAL SET UP.

A second inscription, also from York, records the anguish of a father who believed his daughter was recovering from a severe illness:

TO THE SPIRIT OF THE DEPARTED
CORELLIA OPTATA, 13 YEARS OLD.
O YE HIDDEN SPIRITS, THAT DWELL IN
THE DARK REALM OF THE UNDERWORLD,
WHOM THE FRAIL GHOST SEEKS OUT
AFTER LIFE'S FLEETING DAY. I THE
PITIABLE FATHER OF AN INNOCENT
CHILD, CHEATED BY FALSE HOPE,
LAMENT HER FINAL END. QUINTUS
CORELLIUS FORTIS HAD THIS
MONUMENT PLACED HERE.

Plate 20. *A Roman altar at Haddon Hall, near Bakewell.*

Plate 21. *Divers retrieving a cutstone from the site of the Roman bridge over the Derwent.*

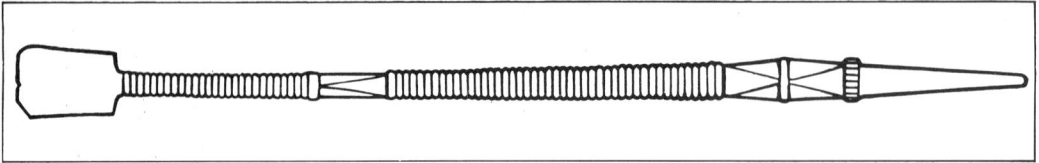

Figure 19. Above: Stylus for writing on wax tablets. Right: Second-century samian bowl found near the Principa. Below: Samian pottery stamps. Opposite page: Figure 20. Decorated samian pottery: (1) first-century, Strutt's Park; (2) second-century, Little Chester (see Figure 11.G). Made by the potter Advocisus, who worked in the period AD160-195.

CRISPI·   TEATOLF   MACRINVS

THE GODS

IN THE pre-Christian era, an extended existence in the realm of the dead offered a dismal prospect. If life on earth was tedious, no relief would be expected in the next world. Appeals to the gods were of no avail in this respect, for they regarded mortals with amused contempt and made no promises of paradise to come. The Greek poet, Sappho, summed the matter up:

'Death is an evil thing.
If it were not so,
Would not the gods die?'

Offerings were made to ascertain the will of the gods and in the hope of avoiding the pitfalls that lay in store for the ordinary mortal.

Requests were made in a business-like manner: 'If I return safely from my journey I will raise an altar to you.' One man who had gambled away his offering of money still dedicated it, relying on the avarice of the god to retrieve it. The aid of the gods was also sought to gain retribution on a thief or a former lover. An example of this sort of appeal is given below:

'May a burning fever seize all her limbs
killing her soul and heart
O gods of the underworld,
break and smash her bones,
choke her,
let her body be twisted and broken'.

42

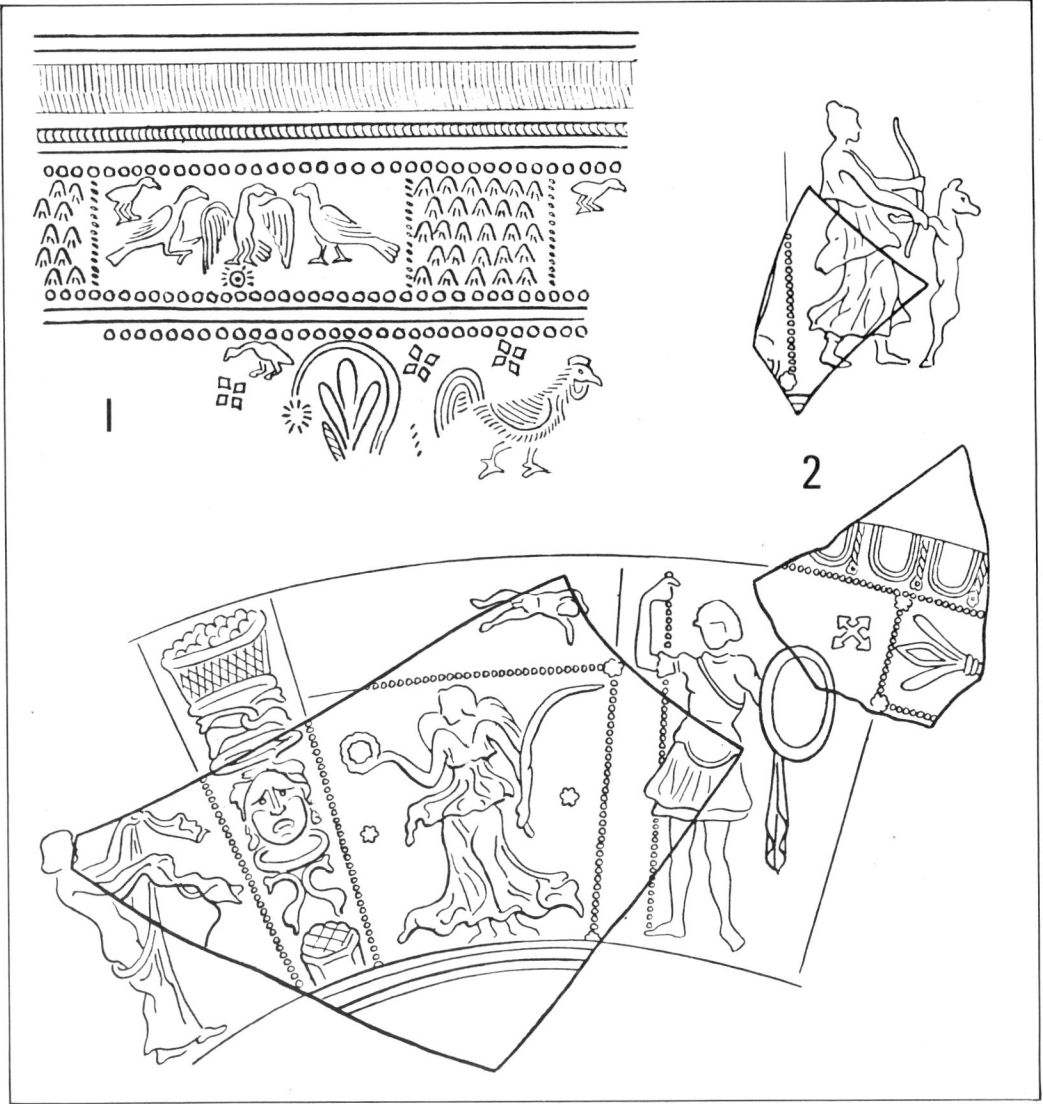

THE MERCURY STONE

A STONE image of a god *(Fig 21.B)*, the only carving to be recovered from Little Chester, was found in the last century by a gardener when digging in a field near the river. It is a block of gritstone, 20in high, roughly trimmed into the shape of a shrine. Within it is a nude figure crudely carved in low relief. For many years it was thought to represent the Roman god, Mercury, but it is more likely to be the horned god of the Brigantes whose cult was blended with that of the Roman deity. The only other possible cult object is the spout of a pottery flagon *(Fig 21.C)*. This was modelled in the shape of a woman's head wearing an elaborate head-dress. Presumably it represents a goddess and, if so, would have been used for ritual purposes at a shrine.

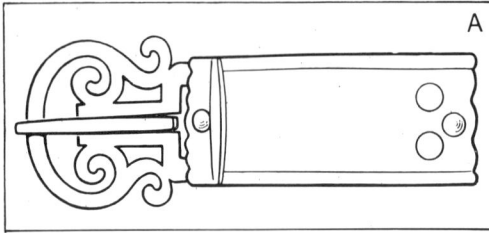

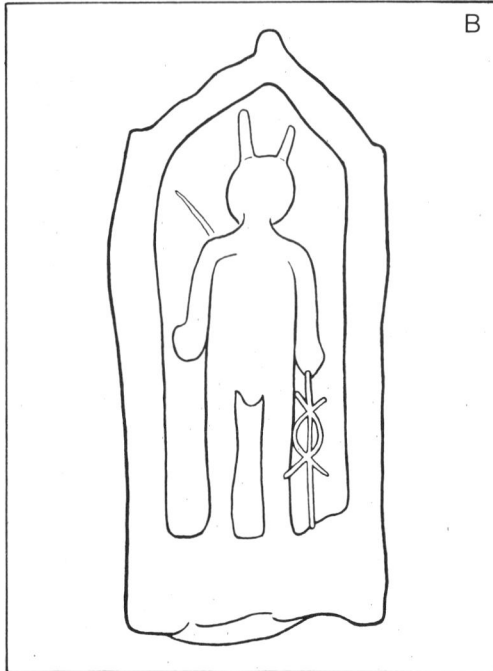

Left: Figure 21. *(A) Belt buckle; (B) The 'Mercury' Stone; (C): Modelled head of flagon.*

THE LATE SECOND CENTURY

MARCUS Aurelius became emperor in AD161 on the death of Antoninun Pius. By inclination he was a philosopher, but his reign, unlike that of his predecessor, was beset with troubles. This required him to spend much of his reign campaigning in Northern Europe. War was threatened in Britain and possibly as a result of the need for troops elsewhere, the Antonine Wall was abandoned and Hadrian's Wall again became the frontier.

In AD180 Aurelius died and his son Commodus became ruler. Leaving the administration of the empire to others, he embarked on a life of pleasure and became besotted with the carriage of the arena, where he fought as a gladiator. In his later years he became demented and believing himself to be a reincarnation of Hercules demanded that he was worshipped as an immortal.

At the beginning of the reign of Commodus, the governor of Britain had been ambushed and killed with all his bodyguards while inspecting the northern frontier. Ulpius Marcellus was sent to lead a punitive expedition to Caledonia. In the brutal war of attrition, Marcellus spared neither himself, his troops, nor his enemy. At its termination the army was in a mutinous mood and he was quickly recalled. His successor, Helvius Pertinax, barely escaped with his life when he was left for dead after a skirmish provoked by an attempt to discipline rebellious troops.

During this period there is evidence of

rebuilding at Little Chester. A series of floors, built one above another, were cut through in an excavation which took place on the site of the Old People's Flats in 1965. The samian pottery associated with the upper floors was manufactured late in the period. Some bowls were made by the potters, Paternus II and Doeccus, and their products were among the last of this ware imported into this country in any quantity before production ceased.

A *Milliaria Equitata* may have been stationed at Little Chester for only a few years. Presumably it would have been required by Marcus Aurelius to help repulse the barbarian invasions on the Continent, or a few years later for the campaign in Scotland. The untidy nature of the upper floors certainly suggests a change of garrison to one of lower status.

THE MURDER OF COMMODUS AND PERTINAX

AFTER several unsucccessful attempts on his life, Commodus was finally murdered in AD192 and the throne offered to Pertinax, who at that time was Prefect of Rome. He accepted with some reluctance as the economy was in a chaotic state. The reforms that he decreed were unpopular and after a reign of 86 days he was murdered by the Praetorian Guard. The guards then put the empire up to auction, announcing that they would place the highest bidder on the throne. Didius Julianus, a senator, offered 25,000 sestertii to each soldier, which was accepted and he was declared emperor.

The populace of Rome, incensed by this shameful procedure sent an appeal to the Governor of Syria, Pescennius Niger, to come to their aid. However, the general Septimus Severus, whose legions were nearer to Rome, moved quickly and occupied the capital. Julianus attempted to negotiate, but after being deserted by the Praetorian Guard was put to death by order of Severus after a reign of only 66 days.

THE RISE OF SEPTIMUS SEVERUS

THE generals now began to fight amongst themselves for control of the empire. The Governor of Britain, Clodius Albinus, saluted as emperor by his troops, was offered by Severus the title of Caesar and this he accepted. This ruse allowed Severus time to attack Niger, whom he defeated in a series of battles and finally killed. After this he declared Albinus to be an enemy of Rome. Albinus withdrew all his legions from Britain and in an initial skirmish with troops loyal to Severus he was successful. The main armies met at Lyons in central France on the 17 February AD197. Although the outcome was often in doubt, Albinus was ultimately defeated and committed suicide. His wife and children were put to death and the bodies of the whole family were thrown into the River Rhone.

THE THIRD CENTURY

SEVERUS was now the undisputed master of the Roman world. To consolidate his position with the soldiery he granted them the legal right of marriage and permitted them to live in civil settlements with their families. The legions of Albinus were ordered back to Britain, where during their absence the Caledonians had broken through Hadrian's Wall and caused extensive damage.

Because of heavy casualties the legions were unable to campaign against these invaders and Virius Lupus, the new governor, had to resort to bribery to induce the tribesmen to leave Roman territory. They subsequently became very bold and looting expeditions occurred with increasing frequency. Finally, in AD208, the governor wrote to Severus stating that the situation was so serious that the presence of the emperor was required. At Rome, Severus received the news with great joy. He considered that his two sons were being corrupted by licentious living and that a hard campaign at the frontier would be an excellent remedy. He set out for Britain immediatley, taking his whole family and staff with him, gathering troops as he went.

The Emperor established himself at York, which for the next three years became the *de facto* capital of the empire. The defences of the north were quickly renovated.

At Little Chester the inner defensive ditch was certainly redug at this time and stone gateways may have replaced wooden ones. With Severus and his staff only a short distance away, the wooden stockade and internal buildings of the fort would have undoubtedly have been put in good order.

The Caledonians, overawed by the presence of the Emperor and the enormous army that he was assembling against them, sued for peace. Severus, however, left the envoys waiting until he had completed his arrangements, then sent them away empty-handed. The campaign started in AD209, and although Severus penetrated to the far north of the island, he could not bring the tribesmen to battle. In the mountainous terrain the Caledonians adopted a policy of guerrilla warfare which inflicted heavy losses on the invaders.

In reply, the Romans systematically laid waste to their lands. The rigours of war eventually broke the health of the Emperor and the campaign, the following summer, was led by his eldest son. A truce was then arranged which was broken in the winter when the Caledonians attacked the garrisons that had been left in their territory. In a rage, Severus began to organize another campaign. The exertion, however, proved fatal. He died at York on 4 February AD211. His final advice to his sons is said to have been *'live in peace together, treat the soldiers well, don't bother about anyone else'*.

CARACALLA

AS SEVERUS had intended, his two sons succeeded to supreme power and reigned jointly. Having no inclination to continue the war, they eventually came to terms with the Caledonians and withdrew the army to Hadrian's Wall. Although named Antoninus, the eldest son is known to this day by the nickname Caracalla (duffle coat) because of his habit of wearing a hooded cloak.

By nature vindictive, he resented sharing power with his brother, Geta, and soon after their return to Rome had him assassinated.

The remainder of the reign of Caracalla, otherwise noted for cruelty and debauchery, is memorable for the one decree which granted Roman citizenship to all free-born people of the empire. In AD217, Caracalla was murdered at the instigation of Macrinus, the Prefect of the Praetorian Guard, a man of humble origin, who was then proclaimed emperor and later killed by the Syrian army after a reign of 14 months.

The decrees on marriage and citizenship resulted in great changes in soldiers accommodation. At Little Chester the barrack blocks were dismantled. If the evidence of the bracelets, necklaces and baby burials found in the third-century levels is taken into account, married quarters were established within the fort at this time. The garrison must also have been greatly reduced, for generous spacing was allowed between buildings.

In some areas within the fort a thick layer of loam has also been encountered, which may also indicate some cultivation. Outside the east gate, a large timber-framed building was constructed which had a roof made of Charnwood slates supported by cross-braced wooden columns. The stone bases for this structure can still be seen. They were uncovered when the site was excavated in 1972 after the railway embankment had been removed.

In front of the building, on the eastern kerb of Ryknield Street, a square-sectioned masonry well was found. It has since been consolidated for display and in June 1980 was blessed during a well-dressing ceremony.

The second half of the third century was a period of instability in the administration of the empire. A raging inflation made the coinage virtually worthless. In the forty years after

Plate 22. *A coin of 'Caracalla'.*

AD244, over fifty emperors or Caesars were proclaimed by the army and raised to the purple from humble origins. Many were murdered within days or months. Despite the unsettled conditions which troubled the Continent, Britain remained peaceful and the frontier tribes remained quiet.

A Continental poet described Britain with envy as 'a land remarkable for its wealth in corn, pasture lands and cattle; full of valuable metals yielding vast revenue'. Order was restored to the rest of the empire when Diocletian was proclaimed emperor in AD285. A competent soldier, he was also an able administrator who introduced a new monetary system and completely reformed the economy. In AD286 he appointed Maximian to share the imperial power as ruler of the western provinces. The Christian faith, which had been gradually spreading throughout the empire, was legislated against as it was considered a menace to the state because of the belief in an authority higher than the emperor.

CARAUSIUS

MAXIMIAN, the western emperor, instructed Carausius the commander of the channel fleet, to clear the seas of Frankish and Saxon pirates. He succeeded in doing this but came under suspicion of diverting retrieved treasure to his own use. Learning that his execution had been ordered, he sailed with his fleet for Britain where he established himself as emperor in AD286. He maintained an independent state for six years until he was murdered by his chief minister, Allectus. Three years later, in AD296, Constantius, the deputy to Maximian, invaded Britain and recovered the province without much difficulty.

THE STONE WALLS OF LITTLE CHESTER

IT WAS during this period that the defences of Little Chester were drastically remodelled. The clay rampart was cut back to receive a stone wall 9ft thick at the base *(Plate 19)*. The wall stood on a foundation composed of six layers of sandstone blocks which was found to be 12ft wide at the west gate. The concrete cored walls would have reached a height of

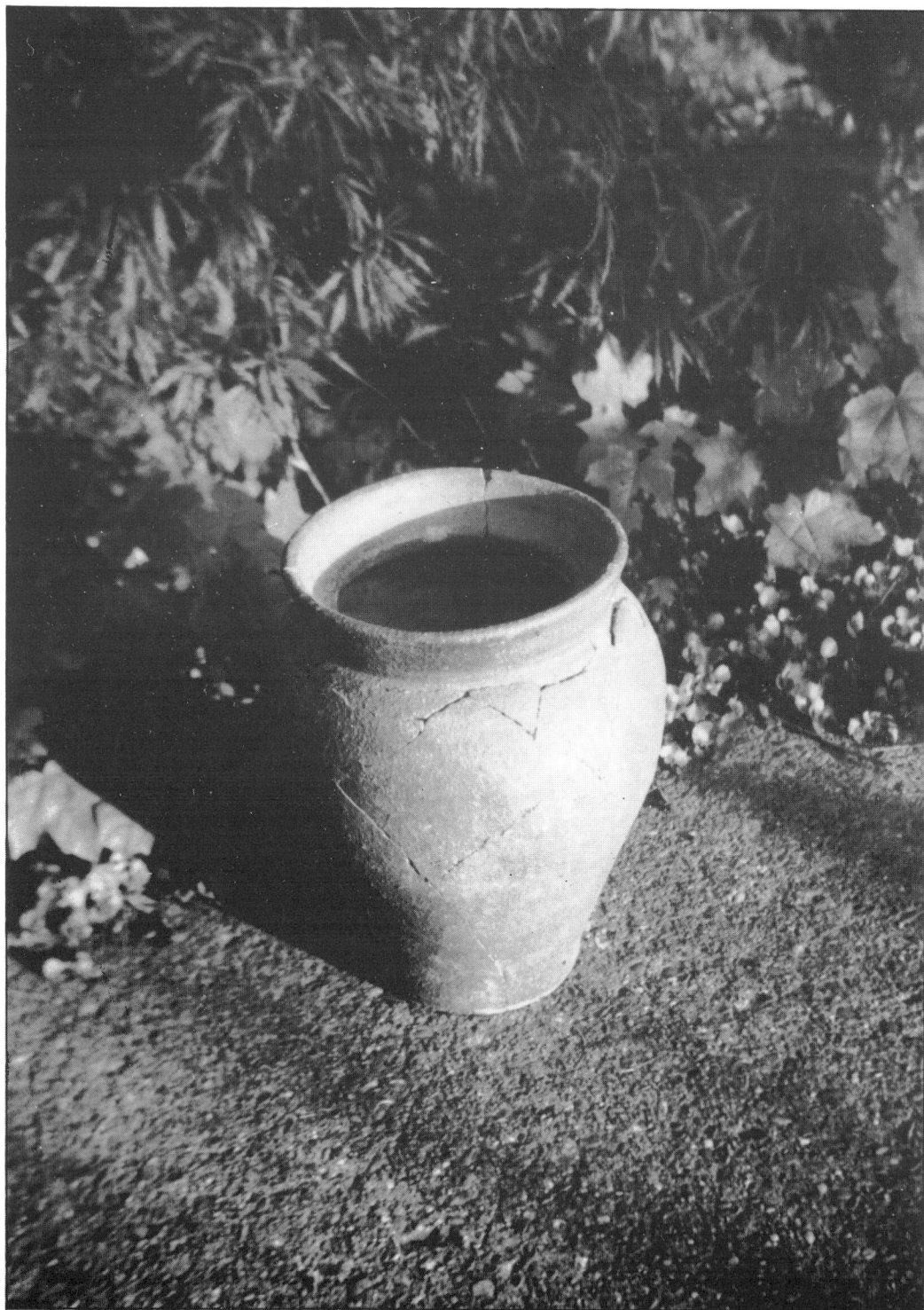

Plate 23. *Derbyshire Ware storage jar.*

Above: Plate 24. *A worked gritstone facing stone from the Derwent, probably from a pier of the Roman bridge.*
Below: Plate 25. *Ripley Salvation Army Band, Whit Tuesday 1933, playing in front of the Hypocaust building on Parker's Piece, Little Chester.*

20ft and represented an enormous amount of stone and expenditure of labour.

It is not clear why defences of such strength were required, presumably they were part of the defence against the central government. In support of this theory is the fact that Carausian coins were found among the waste stone chippings and mortar associated with the construction of the wall.

In December 1904, John Ward carried out a swift but accurate survey of the fort for Francis Haverfield, who was compiling a county history. He gave the dimensions of the fort as 615ft by 540ft. The former dimension was checked across the exposed wall footings in 1968 and found to be 611ft. A wide defensive ditch surrounding the fort was also dug during this period.

THE FOURTH CENTURY

DIOCLETIAN'S policy of shared responsibility at first worked well, but it resulted in as many as five emperors ruling at the same time. Constantius became the senior emperor in AD305, when Diocletian and Maximian retired, but he died a year later at York after successfully repelling an invasion by the northern tribes.

The Caledonians had been so weakened by the devastation of their lands by Severus that it had taken four generations for them to regroup and once again challenge the Romans.

For the first time they are referred to as Picts or 'painted people', which is thought to be a reference to their tattooed skin. A new race of people, who later gave trouble, were the Scots who had migrated from Ireland, at first settling in the western highlands, but eventually overrunning the whole country north of the Roman frontier.

CONSTANTINE THE GREAT

CONSTANTINE, the son of Constanius and his Christian mistress Helena, was proclaimed emperor at York by the troops. This began a long struggle with his co-rulers and it was AD324 before the empire was united under his sole rule. In one crucial battle near Rome, Constantine was convinced that his victory had been achieved through the Divine Intervention of the Christian God. Soon afterwards, in AD313, he issued the Edict of Milan which granted religious toleration to all citizens.

The city of Byzantium, the present Istanbul, was coverted into a new Christian capital; the new Rome. In May AD330, this city was dedicated and called Constantinopolis, but the old name was used to describe the eastern provinces which later became known as the Byzantine empire.

The first half of the fourth century was a

Figure 22. *Parker's Piece pavilion. On the right is the hut which was erected over the Hypocaust building.*

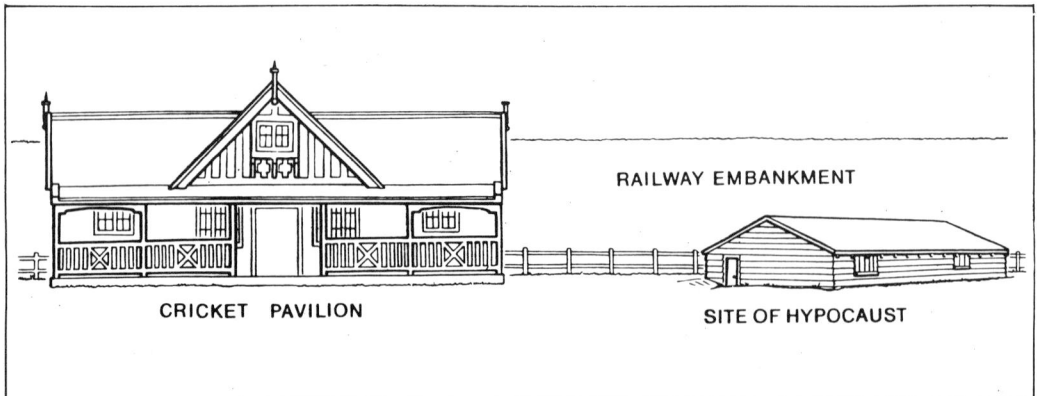

CRICKET PAVILION

RAILWAY EMBANKMENT

SITE OF HYPOCAUST

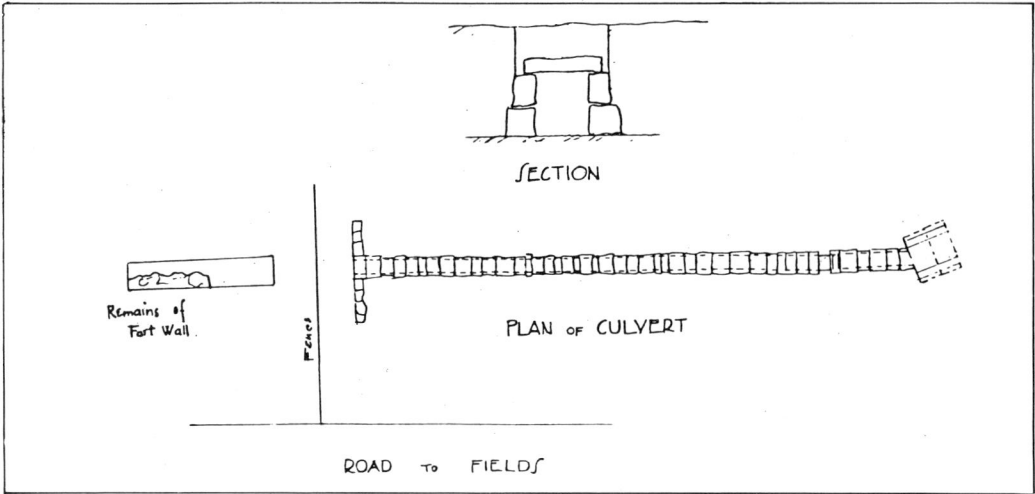

Figure 23. *Sherwin's plan of the culvert, 1926.*

period of great prosperity in Britain, at least for the wealthy. At this time many luxurious houses and villas with mosaics and underfloor heating were built. At Little Chester, the random find of a single purple glass cube, one-inch square, is sufficient to confirm the presence of a mosaic floor of high quality somewhere on the site. A mosaic floor is rumoured to lie under a football pitch in the playing fields to the north of Little Chester, lying about 18in below the surface. A stone culvert, some 90ft long, which drained into the northern defensive ditch may have been associated with this presumed building. The culvert was discovered in 1926 and lies buried on the western side of the tree-lined path crossing Darley Playing Fields *(Fig 23)*.

In 1924, a stone footing was discovered by workmen on the Derby School cricket ground. It proved to be a wing of a substantial building, the bulk of which still lies sealed beneath the railway embankment which forms the southern boundary of the playing field. In the following year, boys of the school uncovered the foundations of a room which had walls 3ft thick.

The overall dimensions are not known but a wall 35ft long is recorded. The building was at first referred to as a bath house and later as a hypocaust building. The remains lie some 30ft to the south-west of the cricket pavilion and when excavated, a considerable amount

of pottery, roofing tiles and painted wall plaster was found. A hypocaust constituted the Roman equivalent of central heating. Hot air from a furnace was ducted under the floor and flowed out via flues set in the thickness of the wall. The floor of the building, which had been supported on some twenty sandstone pillars, had disappeared and only the lower concrete floor remained.

It was evident from the eroded state of the pillars, which were originally 1ft-square, that the heating system had been in use for many years. The construction suggests a fourth-century building and a coin of Gratian (AD367-383) was found lying on the hypocaust floor. The reverse of the coin carried the legend 'Gloria Romanorum' and depicted the standing figure of the emperor holding in his left hand a Christian standard and with his right grasping a kneeling captive by his hair.

THE LATE FOURTH CENTURY

WITHIN the fort many sherds of Oxfordshire ware (a late type of Roman pottery imitating samian ware) have been found. Coins are plentiful up to the end of the century, the latest known to writer are of Valentian II (AD375-392) and Arcadius (AD395).

In AD367 an attack by the Saxons from the south and by the Picts and Scots from the north caused great devastation. Theodosius, a Roman general, succeeded in the following year of clearing the country of the invaders and restoring the defences of Britain. It may have been at this time that two severed heads were thrown down a well which lay outside the defences near to the north-east corner of the fort *(Fig 6)*.

Later in the century, Barbarian pressure on all of the western Roman provinces increased. Britain was weakened by the attempts of usurpers to seize control of the empire. First Magnus Maximus in AD383, and later Constantine III in AD407, withdrew troops from Britain to fight on the Continent, leaving the country open to attack by marauding Angles and Saxons.

THE FIFTH CENTURY

A PLEA to the Emperor Honorius in AD410 for help brought the reply that the cities of Britain would have to undertake their own defence. Soon afterwards Rome was besieged and plundered by the Goths. The unthinkable had happened, the city unconquered for the previous 800 years, the ancient mistress of the world, had fallen. In Britain, centralized government collapsed and coinage was no longer issued. Having no one to turn to, the cities put their defences in order and were at first successful in repulsing the Barbarians and confining them to certain areas. All who could do so now lived behind defensive walls and undoubtedly this was the case at Little Chester.

The Angles, or English as they were later called, had colonized the Trent Valley and for a time at least the Little Chester fort must have been a bastion preventing any further infiltration into Derbyshire. By the middle of the century the Roman way of life began to break down owing to the relentless pressure of the colonists. The Britons, however, continued to resist, although weakened by inter-tribal strife and plague. A long period of fluctuating warfare continued until, at the end of the century, a British victory checked the English advance and stabilized the situation for many years.

THE SIXTH CENTURY

SOON after AD550, the English conquest began again and presumably it was at this time that Little Chester fell into their hands. By the end of the century, most of Britain was under the control of Anglo-Saxon kingdoms and the 'Welsh' (an English word meaning foreigner) were either assimilated or confined to the western parts of the country.

In 1972, at Little Chester, an Anglian cemetery was found by Mr C.Sparey-Green, The burials lay in and around the ruins of the late Roman building at the crossroads outside the east gate of the fort. Seventeen burials were excavated, six of which were women wearing their personal jewellery *(Fig 24)*. The rest were men, two of whom were warriors buried with their shields and spears.

An entry in the Anglo-Saxon Chronicle for AD937 refers back to these early times:

'...the Angles and Saxons came over the broad sea invading Britain from the east. Warriors, eager for fame, proud forgers of war; the Welsh they overcame and for themselves a kingdom won'.

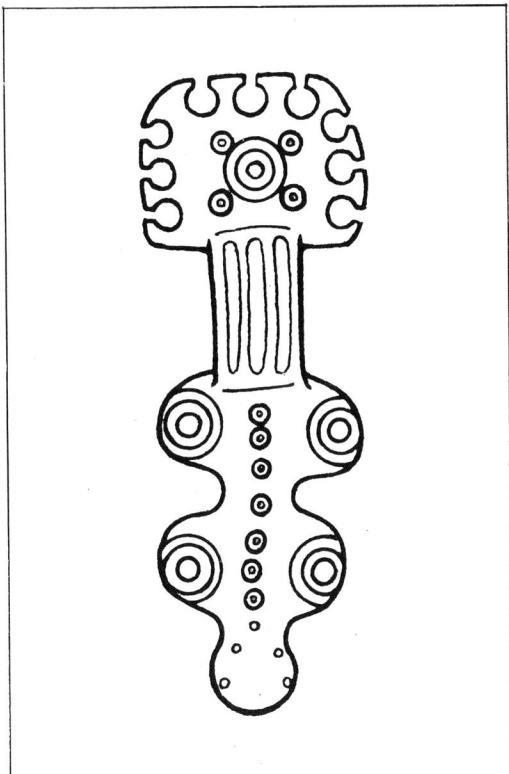

Figure 24. *An Anglo-Saxon bronze brooch, one of a pair, from the grave of an old woman who had been buried at the foot of the Roman fort wall.*

Further information can be obtained from the following journals:

Antiquaries Journal, Vol 51 & Vol 60.
Britannia, Vol XIX & XX.
Derbyshire Archaeological Journals,
Vol LXXXI to the present day.

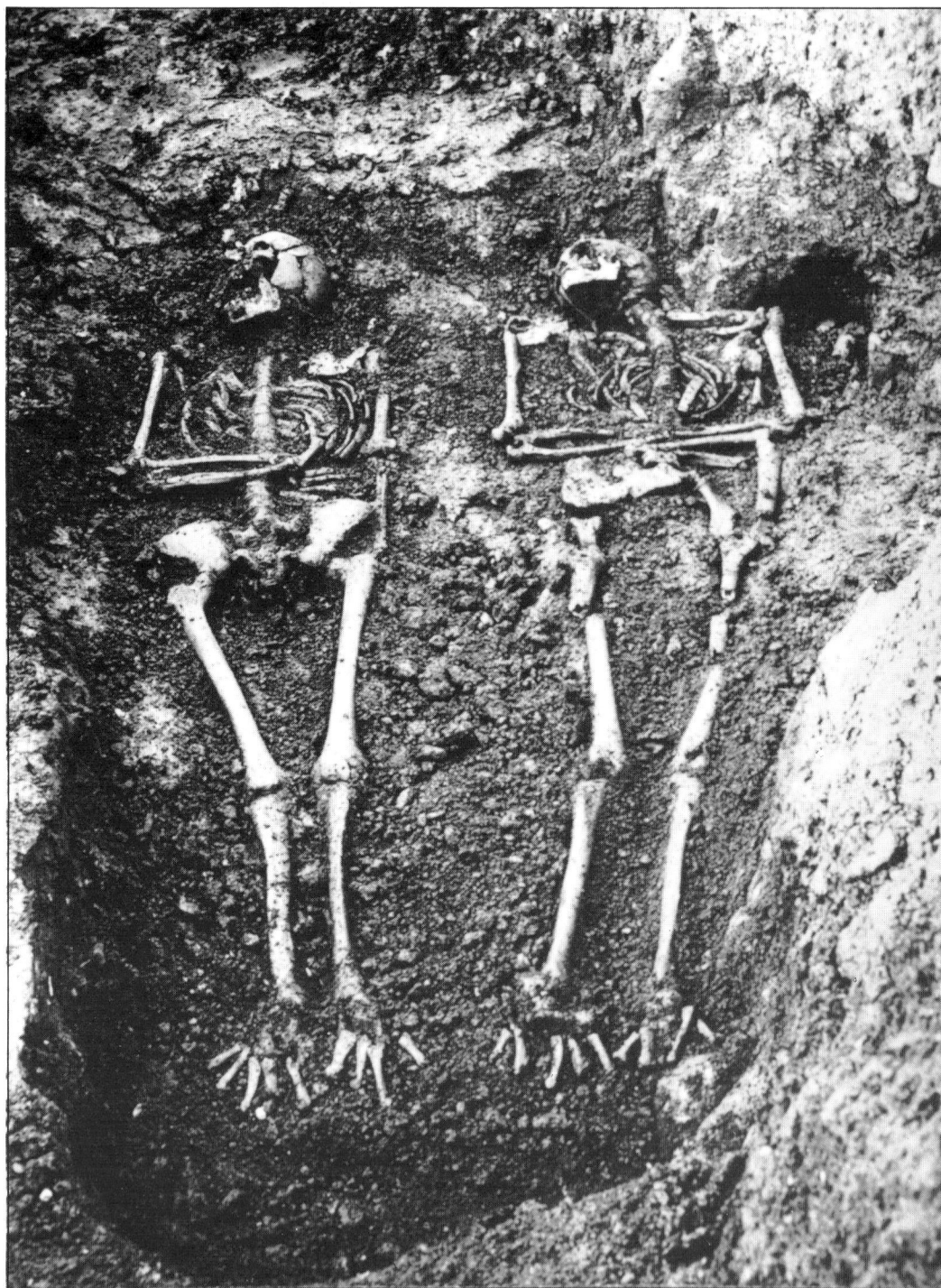

Plates 26-31. *Medieval Christian burials found in the north-west quarter of the Roman fort, 1926. Opposite page (top left) shows the internment of a medieval family group, possibly plague burials. Bottom left shows the exhumation of an Anglo-Saxon woman, sixth-century.*

Above: Plate 32. *A pewter casting depicting, in relief, a nymph riding on a sea-horse. Found in 1966. Below:* Figure 23. *Representation of the original design.*